D1257468

Wellsprings of Renewal

Other Books by Donald G. Bloesch

Centers of Christian Renewal
The Christian Life and Salvation
The Crisis of Piety
The Christian Witness in a Secular Age
Christian Spirituality East and West (Co-author)
The Reform of the Church
The Ground of Certainty
Servants of Christ (Editor)
The Evangelical Renaissance

Wellsprings of Renewal

Promise
in
Christian Communal Life

by
DONALD G. BLOESCH

WILLIAM B. EERDMANS PUBLISHING COMPANY
GRAND RAPIDS, MICHIGAN

Library of Congress Cataloging in Publication Data

Bloesch, Donald G 1928-
  Wellsprings of renewal.

  Bibliography: p. 114.
  1. Monastic and religious orders, Protestant.
I. Title.
BV4405.B47   255'.8   72-93618
ISBN 0-8028-1500-6

To Richard W. Evans,
for encouraging me in community research

Preface

With the new interest in communities, especially among college-age young people, it seems appropriate to give a historical analysis and theological appraisal of community life in Protestantism. In this book I have given special attention to contemporary ventures in community living, particularly those that are evangelically oriented. Many of these communities I have visited personally, some several times. In my estimation the church should not close its eyes to this current manifestation of the Spirit, for communal fellowships may be the new vanguard in the church's mission. Though I myself have chosen that pattern of discipleship in which witness to Christ is made within the structures of the ordinary life, I am keenly aware that effective Christian living within the world needs as its complement signs of separation from the world.

The rise of community life in Protestantism comes at a time when many communities in Roman Catholicism are dissolving or taking on new forms. This phenomenon therefore has considerable ecumenical significance and should be of special interest to those who pray for the unity of the church in our time.

The fact that many of the new communities have their basis in conservative evangelical Protestantism is also of significance, since the traditional alliance of evangelicalism with middle-class values would seem to be overcome. It should also give those who are attracted to radical-secular theology cause for reflection. Perhaps the key to a Christian style of life in a secular age is not new social reforms (though these will still be needed) but personal regeneration. It may be that the heart of any effective social reform is in the inward, spiritual change of perspective, which evangelicals have traditionally called conversion.

In a time when church leaders are lamenting the ebbing away of faith, it is salutary to turn to individuals and groups with spiritual purpose and dedication, men and women in whom God is acting in a mighty, dramatic way. While secular theologians are speaking of the absence of God, the new fellowships of renewal are attesting to His living, redemptive presence.

My first book *Centers of Christian Renewal* was a comparative study of eight contemporary Protestant communities. Other works of mine on the subject of spiritual renewal and the new life in Christ are *The Crisis of Piety* and *The Reform of the Church*. It is my hope that the pioneering efforts reported in this book will prove to be a source of help and encouragement for those who earnestly desire the renewal of the church in our time.

Contents

God always wants to have a place, a community, which belongs to Him really and truly, so that God's being can dwell there. God needs such a place from where He can work for the rest of the world. There must be a place on the earth from where the sun of God's kingdom shines forth.

—*Christoph Blumhardt*

1

Introduction:
The Community Phenomenon

Since the close of the Second World War religious communities have appeared in ever growing numbers in the churches of the Reformation, and the interest in community life shows no sign of abating. Tens of thousands of earnest Christians from every walk of life have been motivated today to come together and live a common life under a common discipline; there is usually a common purse as well. Over sixty thousand women, mostly in Europe, have taken up the religious life; most of these are deaconesses but many others belong to new monastic-type sisterhoods. The West German Protestant church has witnessed the rise of more than twenty thriving experiments in communal living. In America the flowering of community life is especially evident among young people. The newly emerging Jesus movement sees the Christian house or commune as a key means for the nurturing of its youthful converts; there are now several hundred of these communes, most of them in the Far West. New ventures in the common life are also appearing in the Catholic churches as well as in the secular world (cf. the hippie communes). Some communities of Christian renewal (Taizé, Iona, L'Abri) have become centers of pilgrimage for young people.

Most of these new forms of Christian community life signify a marked divergence from the traditional monastic pattern associated with Greek and Roman Catholicism. Instead of withdrawal and detachment from the pressing concerns and needs of the world, the emphasis is now on identification and solidarity with the world in its travail and misery. This is true of recent experiments within the Roman Catholic Church as well as within Protestantism.

A variety of motivations can be detected in the community upsurge. Some communal ventures influenced by the liturgical renaissance have been inspired to forge new forms of worship and Eucharistic devotion. Communities have also arisen out of a need for retreat and silence in a world where deep reflection is becoming ever more difficult. Here we might mention St. Julian's community in England, St. David's Retreat House near Rättvik in Sweden, and St. Augustine's House, a Lutheran monastery near Oxford, Michigan. Many earnest Christians have felt called to come together in order to give a tangible witness to Christian unity. Still others see their role as serving the outcasts and derelicts of society. This is especially true of communal experiments associated with secular-radical theology. Finally, there are those who see their primary vocation in terms of the conversion of the lost by word and deed, but with special emphasis on the proclamation of the Gospel; these can be denominated the evangelical communities. Though it is not unusual for community life to be portrayed as a desirable end in itself, more often it is viewed as a means to a higher end, whether this be service in the world, evangelism, Christian unity and reconciliation, or simply the adoration of God.

The revival of interest in community is a well-known fact, but what is not so well known is that Evangelical Pietism is one of the main sources of the new ventures in community life. Pietism (or evangelical revivalism) is presently under a cloud in avant-garde theological circles, but even in its somewhat impure forms it is proving to be a wellspring of new life in the church. Latter-day Pietism has been accused of being reactionary, of bringing the faith into alliance with bourgeois values, and there is some justification for these criticisms; yet today those

who come out of this tradition are in the vanguard of
what might be considered radical or revolutionary Christianity.

Though the new evangelical communities have a
similar origin, they present a pattern of great diversity. In
England Lee Abbey and Scargill function as centers for
"house parties" where the emphasis is on fellowship
evangelism. The Christ-Bearers (*Christusträger*) in Germany seek to reach the disenchanted among the young
by Christian pop music and street-corner preaching. Jesus
Abbey in South Korea, founded by Archer Torrey,
grandson of the famed R. A. Torrey, was established as a
center of prayer and Christian witness dedicated to
revival in the church of Korea. Bethany Fellowship in
Minneapolis, Minnesota, began as a training center for lay
missionaries. Originally influenced by the Oxford Group
movement, the Daughters of Mary in Denmark and
Sweden have sought to bring the reconciling love of
Christ to lands that have become increasingly secularized.

Founded by Dawson Trotman, the Navigators, which
might be likened to an evangelical religious order,
emphasize personal witnessing and Bible memorization as
tools for spiritual growth. Also deemed very important is
the house ministry in which young Christians are taken
into the homes of members for a limited period of time
and there instructed in the fundamentals of the faith,
including the value and methods of witnessing. In the
home there is complete sharing and brotherhood as new
Christians learn about the Christian life firsthand. The
headquarters of this worldwide movement is Glenn Eyrie
in Colorado Springs, Colorado, where a permanent staff
conducts conferences and training sessions on the Christian mission.

In the house of the Brotherhood of the Cross in Naila,
Germany, married and unmarried persons live together,
working for Christian unity and reconciliation with all
Christian bodies and with all people. The community
maintains especially warm fraternal relations with the

Focalari, a spiritual-life movement within the Roman Catholic Church (see p. 109). The Brotherhood of the Cross is a self-governing body within a wider communal fellowship, the Brethren of the Common Life.

Operation Mobilization, a Christian literature crusade situated mainly in Europe, organizes its young people in gospel teams who live in community, sometimes sharing even clothes and other personal belongings, while engaged in the work of mission. Its crusading zeal recalls to mind the intrepid missionaries of the early church who sallied forth against the Teutonic barbarian tribes, the conquerors of Rome, and compelled them to bow the knee to Jesus Christ.

Equally forthright in their witnessing are the Jesus people. With their literal approach to the Bible and puritanical morality they present a startling contrast and also a sharp challenge to the liberal ecumenical establishment. The concern of the "Jesus freaks," as they are known, is not with the totally immanent God of modern liberal theology, the creative life-force within the world, but with the transcendent, manlike God of biblical faith with whom it is possible to establish a personal relationship. Their open-air mass baptisms, street-corner witnessing, and Jesus rock festivals are increasingly bringing them into the public eye. The traditional monastic disciplines of chastity, obedience, and poverty reappear in the Jesus movement but in a modified form.

Among the new spiritual centers related to this movement in the United States are His Place in West Hollywood, California; the Lighthouse Ranch in Loleta, California; the Beth Nimrah House in Whittier, California; Our Father's Family in Pasadena, California; Solid Rock House in Novato, California; the Lord's Fish House in La Mesa, California; Stone House in Boise, Idaho; the Shiloh Houses in Oregon and other states; the Voice of Elijah in Spokane, Washington; and God's Love in Action in Chicago.

Also worthy of mention are the semi-monastic Children of God, who have maintained houses in Vancouver, southern California, Texas, Washington, and several other states and are now moving into Europe. Despite adverse publicity concerning its militant methods and rigorism, the movement has attracted a growing number of young people disenchanted with the Establishment and now numbers nearly two thousand. The Christian World Liberation Front, with headquarters in Berkeley, California, represents a theology more in the mainstream of Protestant evangelicalism. Much more will be said on the Jesus communal houses as well as on other evangelical communities in the sixth chapter of this book.

The Anabaptist tradition has also spawned many communal experiments, though not all are expressly evangelical. Besides the Hutterites and the Society of Brothers, which are more traditional, newer communities are the Reba Place Fellowship in Evanston and Koinonia Farm in Americus, Georgia. Still more recent are the Fellowship of Hope in Elkhart, Indiana; the Bridge in Newton, Kansas; Fairview Mennonite House in Wichita, Kansas; and Atlanta Fellowship in Atlanta, Georgia. In Ames, Iowa, the Alpha and Omega Fellowship, which has been strongly influenced by revivalistic fundamentalism, carries on a vigorous evangelistic ministry among university students.

The rediscovery of the gifts of the Holy Spirit is another salient mark of the communitarian revival. To be sure, not all the new ventures encourage the spiritual gifts, but they are particularly in evidence in the more evangelical type of community. This is not to imply that these communities are becoming Pentecostal, though a few are moving in this direction. Rather it means that there is now an openness to the charismatic working of the Spirit that has never been present in the mainline churches. Not only the more spectacular gifts such as the discerning of spirits, miracles, tongues, and healings but the traditionally accepted gifts of preaching, teaching, leadership, and service are being given new prominence and emphasis. Communities that seem to be at least somewhat open to the spiritual gifts and where various of these gifts are in evidence include the Brethren of the Common Life, the Brotherhood of Christ, Lee Abbey, Iona, Taizé, the Evangelical Sisterhood of Mary, Jesus Abbey, Bethany Fellowship, the Reba Place Fellowship, Operation Mobilization, Zion's Order, Daystar, and the communal houses of the Jesus movement and the Catholic Pentecostal movement. Because the gifts of the Spirit are so varied, one or more of them can be assumed to be present in virtually all the new communities. Even though many of these groups are distrustful of the spectacular and bizarre, there is a dawning realization that Christian mission is dependent upon spiritual endowment from on high. Most would agree with the position of Bethany Fellowship that the gifts of the Spirit are a tool chest to be used, not gems to be displayed.

It may well be asked why there is such a burgeoning interest in community life at the present time. One reason is that in the age of the lonely crowd people seek relations with one another at a more deeply personal level. They long for intimacy and fellowship. Primary relationships are often missing in the modern family, and this accounts for the fact that many people are drawn to a new kind of family in which the tie is spirit rather than blood. It should also be noted that young people in particular, alarmed at mounting racial, national, and class conflicts, are yearning for and actively seeking the realization of the age-old ideal of the brotherhood of man. This ideal is anticipated in a concrete way in a communal fellowship characterized by mutual trust and love. Again, the contemporary quest for reality and identity, for an experience of the Eternal, is often met in a community that is centered in worship and that is very much aware of its peculiar mission. Men and women in search of God often find Him in the midst of the *koinonia*, the closely knit fellowship of outgoing love.

The local church congregation should, of course,

provide the fellowship that people seek today, but in many cases the congregation has become too large and impersonal, and the reality of the koinonia is lost. Community cannot be realized apart from integrity in worship and unity in basic conviction, but these no longer apply to many churches in which the bond of unity is only social convention. This is why many people today are turning to vibrant para-parochial fellowships like Camps Farthest Out, Young Life, the Yokefellows, and the Cursillo, as well as to spiritually alive communities like Lee Abbey, the Shiloh Houses, Bethany Fellowship, L'Abri, and Taizé. The religious community ideally should be a sign and reminder to the church of what the church itself should be.

The desire for total dedication is also a significant factor in the upsurge of community life today. In a revolutionary age many young people seek to identify themselves with fellowships that are characterized by revolutionary spiritual fervor. The current popularity of evangelistic movements like the Christ-Bearers, Campus Crusade for Christ, L'Abri Fellowship, the Navigators, the Jesus people, the Focalari, and Operation Mobilization is surely to be attributed to their call for total commitment. In a manifesto sent out for the first crusade of Operation Mobilization in the early '60s twenty-four students declared:

> It is true that we are only a small group of Christian young people, yet we have determined by God's grace to live our lives according to the revolutionary teachings of our Master. Within the sphere of absolute, literal obedience to His commands lies the power that will evangelize the world. Outside this sphere is the nauseating, insipid Christianity of our day.

One further reason can be given for the rising interest in communalism. In an age of rootlessness and rapid mobility many people, especially youth, are yearning for stability and permanence, for a place that they can call their home, both in a spiritual and physical sense. The much vaunted model of the modular man, the man who is ever on the go, repels those who recognize the dehumanizing impact of the technopolis and who wish to recover the abiding values of the rural culture where man can be still and close to nature. The Catholic Worker movement upholds what it calls "the Green Revolution," the return to the soil, and this vision is becoming increasingly attractive to many moderns. Not all the new communal experiments, of course, would share this vision.

In this book we shall try to discover the biblical rationale for community life especially as we explore the two kinds of discipleship delineated in Scripture. We shall trace the rise of monastic communities in the Roman Catholic Church, and then concern ourselves with the protest of the Protestant Reformation. Community life came under severe criticism by the mainline churches of the Reformation; the monasteries were practically abolished in those areas where the Reformed faith was dominant. Yet, as we shall show, it was not long before religious communities reappeared in the Reformation churches but in a new form. Contemporary ventures in community life within Protestantism will then be investigated. Finally an attempt will be made to appraise the new spirituality and to point a new direction for community life in the future.

2

Two Patterns of Discipleship

The rise of the religious community in Christianity must be seen against the background of the Scriptural teaching concerning the two types of discipleship. Too often in Protestantism we have been led to view life in a secular vocation as the only legitimate expression of Christian service. The cleric is excepted, but even he is generally expected to live in society as a family man with income and property.

Scripture tells us that all Christians are called to holiness or sainthood. This truth was rediscovered by the Protestant Reformers, Luther and Calvin, and it has been recognized anew by the Second Vatican Council in the document *De Ecclesia*. The goal of evangelical perfection is surely one toward which all Christians should aspire and not merely a religious elite.

At the same time we must acknowledge the complementary truth that not all Christians are called to sainthood in the same way. Not all Christians are called to live apart from family and property, but neither is it a universal requirement that all men have these things.

In biblical and ecclesiastical history two pathways to sanctity can be discerned, and both should be seen as having equal validity in the sight of God. Two patterns of discipleship have arisen, both of which have biblical foundation. On the one hand, there are those who are called to live wholly in the world for the sake of the Gospel, and this entails family life, property, and participation in the affairs of the state even to the extent of serving in the armed forces. On the other hand, some Christians stand under the imperative to fulfill their vocation apart from the world in religious communities or in solitary witness that often entails the renunciation of family, property, and the use of force and violence. Such persons will always be a creative minority, but that they are necessary to the life of the church cannot be denied. In traditional terminology the two types of discipleship are the secular life, i.e., the life of faith in the world, and the religious life.

Neither way to sanctity should be considered higher or more meritorious than the other. One way may be deemed more necessary in certain periods of church history but certainly not morally superior. In the period of the early church the accent was placed upon living against the world and even apart from the world. Most of the early Christians lived a style of life that clearly set them apart from the prevailing mores of the culture; a few retired into the desert and became anchorites as a symbolic protest against a corrupt civilization. Nearly all the early Christians refused to participate in the Roman army not only because this involved homage to the emperor but also because it entailed the shedding of blood.

The Protestant Reformers, on the other hand, called people back into the world in order to change it and bring it more into accord with the teaching of the Gospel. Indeed, in their theology, to be against the world one had to live wholly in it to make his protest effective. The Reformers believed that Christians are called to active combat in the world, not to retirement from the world. Admittedly they did not always give sufficient recognition to the fact that sometimes withdrawal may be necessary for the purpose of deeper penetration into the world.

The two ways of discipleship should be seen as complementary. The church needs both those who separate from the world or from certain practices in the world and those who seek to make their witness wholly in the world. It should be recognized that all discipleship entails inward separation, an inward sacrifice. Those who have the goods of this world should not let these things dominate their lives, for single-minded devotion is to be given only to God (cf. I Cor. 7:29-31). Those who are blessed with marriage and family should nevertheless not let family cares take precedence over the kingdom of God (cf. Lk. 14:26). Luther attested to the costly character of all discipleship in these words from his great hymn *A Mighty Fortress:*

> Let goods and kindred go,
> This mortal life also;
> The body they may kill;
> God's truth abideth still,
> His kingdom is forever.

Those who make the outward sacrifice, that is, who actually give up goods and kindred *de facto,* or who give up reputation and worldly honor out of fidelity to Christ, become potential signs of the sacrifice that is required of all Christians. The church has ever regarded the highest sacrifice as martyrdom; the passion and victory of Jesus Christ become visible in the lives of those who suffer for the faith publicly, whether they live in society or apart from it. When religious celibacy, voluntary poverty, or martyrdom become fashionable, however, the value of the sign diminishes, and worldliness then prevails in the guise of religiosity.

In the Bible the two types of discipleship are very much in evidence. In the Old Testament those who feel impelled to live apart from the world are represented by the Nazarites, the Rechabites, and the sons of the prophets. Many of these people lived in companies or bands and even on occasion in communities separated from ordinary society. These prophets and ascetic nomads were regarded as holy men in ancient Israel, but their holiness was marked more by charismatic qualities

than by ethical obedience. Monastic community life did
not appear in Israel until the Essenes in the inter-
testamental period. Jeremiah was required to give up
marriage, but this was considered highly exceptional and
one of the heaviest sacrifices in Old Testament religion.
He saw himself as a prophet of doom and his celibacy as a
sign that the old institutions had been abandoned by God
and were passing away.[1] Other prophets such as Elijah
and Elisha were involved in a ministry that entailed
separation from Israelite society at least for a period. At
times they lived a life of virtual poverty, but nothing is
said of celibacy (although this possibility must not be
discounted). In Second Isaiah we find a witness to the
value of celibacy that associates it with the dawning of a
new aeon: "For thus says the Lord: 'To the eunuchs who
keep my sabbaths, who choose the things that please me
and hold fast my covenant, I will give in my house and
within my walls a monument and a name better than sons
and daughters; I will give them an everlasting name which
shall not be cut off' " (Is. 56:4, 5).

In the New Testament the life of renunciation and
poverty can be discerned in the company of the twelve
and also in the seventy who were sent out two by two as
missionaries without purse, bag, or sandals (Lk. 10). It
should be recognized, however, that nothing is said about
vows of permanent celibacy, and we know that many of
the disciples were married. Surely John the Baptist, who
was probably influenced by the Essenes, as well as
missionaries like Paul, Silas, and Barnabas, exemplify the
separated life (including the life of celibacy). Community
life in the New Testament church can be seen in the
congregation of Jerusalem, which practiced common
ownership, and in the community of widows mentioned
by the apostle (I Tim. 5).

The Scriptures also uphold the discipleship that is

[1] See Lucien Legrand, *The Biblical Doctrine of Virginity* (N.Y.: Sheed and
Ward, 1963), pp. 25-36.

lived out in the world. The patriarchs—Abraham, Isaac, and Jacob—all had families and the goods of life and yet lived lives that were regarded as exemplary in the sight of God. The same is true of Moses, Aaron, the judges and kings of Israel, and many of the prophets. In the New Testament we can point to the disciples of Jesus, most of whom were probably married (I Cor. 9:5, 6).

Jesus can be regarded as exemplifying both types of discipleship in that He lived apart from family and property and yet lived wholly in the midst of society. It is true that He often withdrew from the multitudes for prayer, but He always returned in order to minister to people. He was even accused of being a winebibber and glutton because He did not practice the asceticism characteristic of the disciples of John the Baptist and traditional holy men of Israel. He was completely in the world and yet not of the world. He gave His blessing to both marriage and celibacy and saw both of these states in terms of service to the kingdom of God (Mt. 19:3-12). He required virtual poverty from one rich man (Mt. 19:16-22), but He approved of Zacchaeus' giving up only half of his goods to the poor (Lk. 19:1-10). To be sure, Zacchaeus also pledged to use the remainder of his wealth to help those whom he defrauded, but we can assume that he still had enough for himself and his family. Again we read that Jesus even encouraged His disciples to use "unrighteous mammon" in His service (Lk. 16:9), thereby pointing to the truth that money and property also have a place in the Christian vocation. One of His followers, Joseph of Arimathea, though rich (Mt. 27:57), was deemed a "good and righteous man" (Lk. 23:50). This is not to discount the firm conviction of Jesus and also of the New Testament church that riches can be one of the gravest stumbling blocks to a life of discipleship.

Mary, the mother of our Lord, also typifies both types of discipleship. She lived in a family, but she also dedicated herself wholly to the service of her son. Biblical scholars tell us that she was probably widowed at an early age, and this accounts for the fact that she was told by Jesus to make her home with the disciple John (Jn. 19:26, 27). Moreover, we read that she was in the upper room at the first Pentecost, and therefore she is to be numbered among the first missionaries of the church. Mary lived in the world and yet apart from the world, since her heart was fixed upon heavenly things (Lk. 2:19). She is to be honored not so much for her virginity as for her constant fidelity to her son and Savior, Jesus Christ.

A danger appears when one type of discipleship is elevated above the other. In the period of the early church this danger became very real when martyrs and confessors were regarded as more holy than ordinary Christians. At the same time virginity came to be adulated, partly in reaction against the moral decadence of the Graeco-Roman world. We can also see in this period the emergence of anchorites and later of monks who separated themselves from society for the purposes of prayer and meditation. Celibacy came to be considered a surer path to sanctity than marriage. Marriage was relegated to the order of nature whereas celibacy was seen to be in the order of grace. John Cassian held that married people are unable to reach the heights of contemplation. In the opinion of Jerome a married couple can live a Christian life only if they abstain from intercourse. He did not deny that saints can be found among widows, but then they are no longer wives.

A dual standard of morality arose in which the "religious life" was seen to be higher and more worthy in the sight of God than the ordinary life. Those who would give themselves wholly to the kingdom were encouraged to follow the counsels of perfection—celibacy, poverty, and obedience. The ordinary Christians, that is, those who chose to live partly in the old aeon, were advised simply to obey the commandments. Thomas Aquinas did not denigrate marriage but regarded it as of less worth than virginity. He held that since the contemplative life immediately and directly pertains to the love of God, it is therefore more meritorious than the active life.[2] That marriage was made into a sacrament by the church testifies to the fact that Catholic theology continued to see marriage as ordained by God and as a veritable means of grace. On the other hand, by sacramentalizing marriage the church elevated it into the realm of the spiritual, thereby implying that there is a deficiency in the physical or material side of marriage.

The community life that took form in the early middle ages was that of the enclosed community devoted primarily to prayer and contemplation. Such were the Augustinians, the Benedictines, and later the Cistercians and the Carmelites. In the later middle ages new forms of community life emerged that signified a synthesis of the contemplative and active life. Here we should mention the Franciscans and Dominicans, who boldly carried the Gospel into the world. Yet even in these orders the idea remained that the religious life is a higher or more worthy form of life than ordinary life in the secular realm. Thomas Aquinas even contended that by entering the religious life "a man obtains remission of all his sins."[3]

The spirituality of the religious orders was tainted by a dualistic asceticism inherited from Platonic mysticism. This criticism stands despite the fact that such spiritual leaders as Augustine reminded the church that the seat of sin is not in the body but in the will of man. That Roman Catholic thought and piety were colored by Platonic philosophy resulting in a denigration of the world is affirmed by the Jesuit scholar Hans Urs von Balthasar: "The patristic period viewed contemplation as a participation in heaven, as an end in itself, and considered ordinary Christian living as little more than a preparatory

[2] Thomas Aquinas, *Summa Theologica* (N.Y.: Benziger, 1947), II-IIae, Q. 188, art. 2, 6. Thomas held that the mixed or apostolic life is preferable to contemplation per se, though the apostolate must be grounded in contemplation.

[3] Thomas Aquinas, *Summa Theologica*, II-IIae, Q. 189, art. 3, p. 2008.

phase, a means of attaining the necessary purity of heart, while the Middle Ages regarded it as a kind of inferior receptacle into which the exuberant riches of contemplation discharged themselves."[4]

If the Catholic Church had difficulty in affirming the validity of secular vocations, this is even more true of various heretical groups that appeared in the early church and medieval periods. The Montanists of the second and third centuries, in anticipation of the end of the world, enjoined celibacy for those who would be perfect, forbade second marriages, and instituted fastings and abstinence from meat. Tertullian, after he became a Montanist, made a distinction between pneumatics or Spirit-filled men and psychics or those who live by animal standards. Anyone who followed a secular calling in the world was regarded as apostate.

In the eleventh century the western world witnessed the emergence of the Cathari, who denied the goodness of creation and stressed the necessity for liberation from the bonds of the flesh. The Cathari distinguished between the ordinary Christian and the *perfectus* who eschews marriage, oaths, war, and the possession of property. The perfect Christian even avoids eating meat, milk, or eggs, since they are products of the sin of reproduction. This heresy has its source in Manichaeism and Platonism, which have constantly imperiled the biblical roots of the faith.

It should be recognized that evangelical voices constantly made themselves heard in the Roman Catholic Church in protest against a double standard of morality. Johann Tauler maintained that even a shoe cobbler could through his work give glory to God. Teresa of Avila insisted that Marthas are as necessary as Marys and that the active and contemplative life need to be held in balance. Meister Eckhart's view was that our works in no

---

[4] Hans Urs von Balthasar, *Prayer*. Trans. A. V. Littledale (N.Y.: Sheed and Ward, 1961), p. 228.

way serve to induce God to give to us or to do anything.

In the Roman Catholic Church today traditional spirituality is under critical reappraisal. The Second Vatican Council as well as many Catholic teachers and theologians seek to break through the double standard of morality that characterized so much spirituality in the past. The Council reminds us that every Christian has an apostolic vocation. Dorothy Day maintains that the counsels of perfection are mandatory for all believers. In the view of Hans Küng Christians everywhere are summoned to live according to the spirit of the counsels even in the secular states of life.

New forms of community life are arising within Catholicism that seek to carry the light of the Gospel into the midst of the world. We might mention here the Glenmary Sisters, who have recently undergone drastic reorganization, the Opus Christi Brothers, the Community of Pope John XXIII, the Community of the Servant of Man, the Fides Community, the Sisters for Christian Community, the Vineyard, the Martin Luther King Community, the Little Brothers and Sisters of Jesus, the Focalari, the Order of the Ark, the hospitality houses of the Catholic Worker movement, and secular institutes such as the Opus Dei and the Grail Society. Attention should also be given to the Missionaries of Charity of Mother Teresa, whose ministry to the dying and hopeless, begun in Calcutta in 1950, now extends to many nations. The plight of the world and service to the needy are looming much more significant in contemporary Catholic spirituality than the mystical contemplation of the ground of being. There is still a real place in Catholic religious life for separation from the spirit and pursuits of the world, but the accent is now on maintaining spiritual integrity while living very much in the world.

3

The Protest of the Reformation

Against the dominant spirituality of their time the Reformers—Luther, Calvin, Zwingli, and others—upheld the biblical theme of the universal call to sanctity. All Christians, whatever their state in life, are required to aim for the highest standard, namely, perfect love. We are all called to share in the priesthood of Christ and to enter into His holiness. It has been said that Calvin sought to make the world into a monastery. Zwingli built a virtual theocracy in Zurich, and the aim of the Puritans was to create holy commonwealths in which every area of life would be brought under the revealed law of God.

The Reformers remind us that the Christian life does not of itself save us; rather it is the cardinal evidence and fruit of our salvation. In their view the justification of God is not contingent upon the sanctification of man; the latter is the consequence of divine justification. The two fundamental motivations for living the Christian life are the desire to glorify God and gratefulness for what He has done for us in Jesus Christ. Reformation theology also recovered the Scriptural truth that the primary means of grace is not the Christian life but the proclamation of the Gospel, although the two should always be conjoined.

In the theology of the Reformation the real sacrifice is inward, and our mode of life is a fruit and sign of our interior relationship with God. This truth had been perceived by Meister Eckhart many years prior to the Reformation: "Indeed, if a man gave up a kingdom, or even the whole world, and still was selfish, he would have given up nothing. If, however, he denies himself, then whatever he keeps, be it wealth, honor, or anything else, he is free from it all."[1] It should be recognized that the Reformers themselves made outward sacrifices as well. Luther not only broke with his immediate family when he entered the monastery, but he broke in addition with his ecclesiastical family, the church, when he reentered the world. His sacrifices remind us that loyalty to Jesus Christ takes precedence over all temporal loyalties.

The protest of the Reformers against the religious communities of their time is of special interest to us. Both Luther and Calvin declared themselves opposed to monasticism as it then existed in the Roman Catholic Church. Their principal criticism was that the monastic life was seen to be more meritorious than ordinary Christian living. Monastic spirituality was actually a type of works-righteousness that stood in contradiction to the evangelical message of justification by free grace. They also complained that the sacrament was given more significance than the Word in monastic communities and that Christian liberty was forfeited by the codes and rules that governed the monasteries. Still another criticism was that the Bible nowhere requires men to place themselves under vows of perpetual celibacy and poverty.

It should be remembered that the monasteries had for some time been under fire from sensitive spirits in the Catholic Church, mainly because their excessive wealth and cultural prestige had drained them of spiritual fervor and also promoted growing laxity in discipline. The Reformers likewise complained of the worldliness of the monasteries, but they located the core of this worldliness in the doctrine of merit or works-salvation, which in their eyes signified an accommodation to human pride and self-will. Luther had been a monk in the monastery of

---

[1] Raymond Bernard Blakney, trans. and ed. *Meister Eckhart* (N.Y.: Harper, 1941), p. 5.

Augustinian hermits in Erfurt where a high level of discipline was maintained, but he saw that the very purpose of monastic life in his day made a compromise with worldly values inevitable. This is not to say that the concept of justification by grace was totally absent in the prevailing theology of that time, but it was united with a belief that human cooperation is a condition for the working of grace, and consequently the biblical emphasis on free grace was obscured by a synergistic orientation.[2]

Again, the Protestant Reformation broke through the dualistic asceticism of the later medieval Catholic spirituality and recovered the doctrine of the goodness of creation. The antithesis, according to the Reformers, is not between spirit and nature but rather between the holy God and man the sinner. Sin, moreover, is not a deficiency or privation but a revolt of man against the will of God. The Reformers concurred in the judgment of the apostle that self-abasement and severity to the body "are of no value in checking the indulgence of the flesh" (Col. 2:23). The seat of man's perversion is spiritual, and what man needs is a spiritual conversion. Catholic mysticism was not wholly oblivious to these truths. Meister Eckhart had said that the body of man was given to him in order to purify the soul. And Fénelon, the noted French mystic who bridged the seventeenth and eighteenth centuries, contended that man must renounce the soul as well as the body. Even so, a metaphysical dualism penetrated deeply into the piety of the cloister, and the Protestant Reformers vigorously protested against it out of fidelity to Scripture.[3]

Yet despite their aversion to the monasticism of their time the Reformers did not censure the principle of religious community life. Indeed, Calvin appears to look

[2] See Philip S. Watson, *The Concept of Grace* (Philadelphia: Muhlenberg, 1959).

[3] One devotional classic of the later middle ages affirms: "For by its nature every physical thing is farther from God than any spiritual." Clifton Wolters, ed. and trans. *The Cloud of Unknowing* (Baltimore: Penguin, 1967), p. 108.

with favor upon the type of monasticism advocated by Augustine, who saw communities as a leaven within the larger church. Nor did Luther fail to recognize the value of the monasteries in the history of the church:

> I certainly do not say that I would condemn the ceremonies of . . . monasteries; for this was the first discipline of the religious, that he who enters a monastery learns to obey his superior, not to labor for himself but to serve everyone in every way. Truly it was the monasteries that served as schools for the exercise and perfection of Christian liberty.[4]

As late as 1538 he declared:

> I should especially like to see the rural monasteries and those that have been endowed stay to take care of noble persons and poor ministers. Nor have I proposed anything else from the beginning. From such monasteries suitable men can then be chosen for the church, the state, and economic life.[5]

Although declaring themselves in opposition to vows of perpetual celibacy, the Reformers allowed for the celibate life. They admitted on occasion that celibacy has a practical but not a moral advantage over marriage. Martin Bucer included celibacy among the special gifts or charisms of the Spirit. On the whole, however, the Reformers viewed celibacy as a gift that is highly exceptional and were unable to see it as an alternative life vocation to marriage.

It is well to note that the Second Helvetic Confession placed a high value on celibacy:

> Those who have the gift of celibacy from heaven, so that from the heart or with their whole soul are pure and continent and are not aflame with passion, let them serve the Lord in that calling, as long as they feel endued with that divine gift; and let them not lift up themselves above others, but let

[4] Martin Luther, *Luther's Works*. Vol. XIV. Ed. Jaroslav Pelikan (St. Louis: Concordia, 1958), p. 301.
[5] Martin Luther, *Luther's Works: Table Talk*. Vol. 54. Ed. and trans. Theodore G. Tappert (Philadelphia: Fortress, 1967), p. 312.

> them serve the Lord continuously in simplicity and humility
> (I Cor. 7:7 ff). For such are more apt to attend to divine
> things than those who are distracted with the private affairs
> of a family.[6]

In general, the churches of the Reformation frowned upon monasticism. And yet many of their leaders and scholars saw the place for communities whose aim would be to educate pastors and church workers. In these communities there might be a place for "permanent" members who would be employed to train those who would give themselves to the service of the church. Some "confessional texts" even allowed for this possibility. For example, in the Wittenberg Articles of 1536 we find this statement:

> If certain men who are capable of living a life under a rule
> prefer to pass their lives in the cloister, we do not reprove
> them so long as their doctrine and worship remain pure and
> they consider the practices of monastic life as things
> indifferent. We are convinced that numerous authentic
> Christians of sound spirituality have lived exemplary lives in
> monasteries. It is even to be wished that such cloisters should
> exist, occupied by learned and devout men, where the study
> of Christian doctrine can be pursued for the greater good of
> the Church. These might then be a place where young people
> are instructed not only in doctrine but also in the ordered
> devotional life.[7]

Despite the door that was opened by the Reformation to an evangelical community life, the children of the Reformation have for the most part failed to rise to this opportunity, though, as we shall see, new ventures in this direction are now being made. The secular or ordinary life in the world has generally been regarded as infinitely superior to the religious or cloistered life. Though it is acknowledged that all Christians are called to whole-

[6] Arthur C. Cochrane, ed. *Reformed Confessions of the 16th Century* (Philadelphia: Westminster, 1966). The Second Helvetic Confession, Ch. XXIX, p. 298.

[7] George Mentz, ed. *Die Wittenberger Artikel Von 1536* (Leipzig: Deichert'sche Verlagsbuchhandlung, 1905), p. 74.

hearted commitment to Christ, sufficient recognition has not been given to the truth that some Christians (besides the clerics) may well be called to full-time church service and that this may entail a life of simplicity and renunciation.

In many Protestant churches marriage has practically become mandatory for both clergy and laity, and the ascetic protest against the values of a mundane culture is no longer heard. In contemporary secular Protestantism the sacred and profane are practically identified, and the mission of the church is envisaged wholly in terms of this world. The state of marriage itself is threatened today, since institutional religion seems unable to withstand the new sex and fertility cults of our time. Present-day Protestantism sorely needs a revival of the asceticism of the New Testament if it is not to succumb completely to a hedonistic, secularistic culture. Such asceticism, which consists in sin-denial rather than world-denial per se, does not cancel out marriage but gives it a new meaning and direction while at the same time allowing for the alternative of celibacy in the service of the kingdom. In this kind of perspective family life is not negated but subordinated to the requirements of the wider family of God.[8]

It was the increasing secularization of modern Protestantism that moved Soren Kierkegaard in nineteenth-century Denmark to yearn for the recovery of the monastic life as a sign and witness of the kingdom that stands over against the world. He declared: "Back to the monastery out of which broke Luther—that is the truth—that is what must be done."[9] He made clear, however, that this does not mean a capitulation to the

[8] It should be noted that the relativization of the family does not mean its destruction but its preservation. The absolutizing of married love or of sexual love spells disaster for the family. Unless Eros is transformed by Agape and placed in the service of God and His kingdom it becomes idolatrous and self-destructive.

[9] Soren Kierkegaard, *The Journals of Soren Kierkegaard*. Ed. and trans. Alexander Drew (London: Oxford U. P., 1951), p. 502.

pope and a return to Catholicism. In his view, "The fault with the Middle Ages was not monasticism and asceticism, but that worldliness had really conquered because the monk paraded as the exceptional Christian." Moreover, the suffering that he saw as authentically Christian was not self-mortification in a cloister but persecution for holding up the Gospel of Christ before the world. Kierkegaard was not sounding a call to repristination but rather pointing to a new kind of community life that would be at the same time both catholic and evangelical.

The liberal Lutheran theologian Adolf Harnack also lamented the virtual disappearance of the ascetic protest in the Evangelical churches of his day:

> Every community stands in need of personalities living exclusively for its ends. The Church, for instance, needs volunteers who will abandon every other pursuit, renounce "the world," and devote themselves entirely to the service of their neighbour; not because such a vocation is "a higher one," but because it is a necessary one, and because no Church can live without also giving rise to this desire. But in the evangelical Churches the desire has been checked by the decided attitude which they have been compelled to adopt towards Catholicism. It is a high price that we have paid; nor can the price be reduced by considering, on the other hand, how much simple and unaffected religious fervour has been kindled in home and family life.[10]

Neither Kierkegaard nor Harnack took sufficiently into consideration the para-parochial fellowships (conventicles, missionary societies, and deaconess institutes) that came out of Evangelical Pietism and that manifested the same kind of total dedication characteristic of the older monasticism at its best. Nor did they recognize the analogy between the monastic orders and the Evangelical sect groups which indeed have functioned as vanguards in the life of the church and which have comprised the growing edge of Protestantism. They might also have

---

[10] Adolf Harnack, *What Is Christianity?* Trans. Thomas Bailey Saunders. Introduction by Rudolf Bultmann (N.Y.: Harper, 1957), p. 288.

considered such monastic-type communities as Ephrata, Herrnhut, and Trevecka, all of which arose out of the evangelical revival and exerted a wide influence for a time. Nevertheless their criticisms of the very pronounced tendency, especially in historical Protestantism, to obscure the fact that there are two patterns of discipleship are for the most part well made.

Reformation Protestantism was compelled to turn its back on community life because this pattern of life seemed to be allied with a system of works-righteousness that was contrary to Scripture. Yet the deep-felt yearning in the human spirit for the kind of consecration the monasteries had symbolized could not long remain stifled, and new ventures in communal life began to make their appearance within the churches of the Reformation, though such ventures were not widely accepted. It was not until the period of the evangelical revivals that a more positive attitude developed toward religious communities, despite continuing opposition.

4

Attempts to
Recover Community Life

Despite the censure of monastic life by the Reformers, many attempts have been made within Protestant history to found religious communities, and some of these have been successful, at least for a time. Only a few have been accepted by the mainstream of Protestantism; others have become sectarian and also utopian and have thereby diluted rather than strengthened the catholic substance of the Evangelical churches.

The Möllenbeck monastery near Rinteln in northwest Germany is one of the first communities to appear within Protestantism. It was originally Augustinian, but in 1558, under the direction of its prior, Father Hermann Wenig, it transferred its allegiance to the Reformation. The faith and practice of the convent were modified in accordance with evangelical (Lutheran) theology. Anything in the liturgy that smacked of the cult of the saints was suppressed, and the idea of the mass as a sacrifice was abandoned. The monastery actually began to prosper as an evangelical community, and the number of novices increased quite notably. A Catholic scholar writes: "If the monastery had few novices in the years preceding its reform, and exercised only a moderate influence in its area, after its reform it became, in contrast, very powerfully influential. The prior of the convent was besieged for advice by callers of every stripe."[1] Yet the

[1] Francois Biot, *The Rise of Protestant Monasticism*. Trans. W. J. Kerrigan (Baltimore: Helicon, 1963), p. 66.

monastery could not survive the bitter controversies engendered by the Thirty Years' War, and it finally died out in the later seventeenth century.

Two other survivals of Catholic monasticism within Lutheranism should be noted.[2] The cloister at Loccum had originally been a Cistercian monastery (founded in 1163), but in 1593 it was reformed in the light of Lutheran theology. Vows were no longer required, but celibacy remained an obligation. Gradually the number of prayer services was reduced from seven to three in line with Lutheran liturgical practice. The community still referred to itself as a Cistercian cloister, and the rule of St. Benedict continued to be observed. A seminary for pastors was instituted in 1792, but the convent remained a separate entity until the later nineteenth century.

At the convent of Marienberg in Helmstedt, formerly an Augustinian cloister for nuns, the Lutheran doctrine came to be accepted in 1569, though not without some opposition. The convent was gradually transformed into an evangelical community for single women. One of the local clergy was designated as the dean of the cloister to supervise regular worship. In the nineteenth century, partly through its contacts with the deaconesses of Neuendettelsau, the convent appropriated the piety and concerns of the Inner Mission movement. In this same period a hospital, a school for girls, and a public school for the surrounding community were established in the cloister. Six sisters still remain at Marienberg and conduct daily worship as well as religious retreats.

The Anabaptist movement, which became prominent in the sixteenth century, made a place for religious communities, but there were marked departures from the traditional monastic form of communal life. Deaconesses were present among the Mennonites from the very beginning, and in the nineteenth and early twentieth

[2] See Frederick S. Weiser, *The Survival of Monastic Life in Post-Reformation Lutheranism*. S.T.M. thesis. Lutheran Theological Seminary, Gettysburg, Penn., 1966.

centuries deaconess houses were founded in several countries including Germany, Holland, Russia, and the United States. Community life was also practiced by the Hutterites, who were comprised of families that came together for the purpose of sharing goods and production. Anabaptist spirituality is reflected in our time in such communities as the Society of Brothers (the Bruderhof), the Hutterian Brethren, the Reba Place Fellowship in Evanston, Illinois, and to a lesser degree Koinonia Farm in Americus, Georgia (see pp. 78f.).

The rise of Evangelical Pietism presaged a new era in Protestant history.[3] Pietism had its roots primarily in the Protestant Reformation, but also partly in Catholic mysticism and the evangelical revivalism of the Anabaptists. Whereas the Reformers had placed the accent upon justification, the Pietists gave special attention to regeneration and sanctification. Among the guiding lights of German Pietism were Philip Jacob Spener, August Francke, Johann Albrecht Bengel, and Count Nicolaus von Zinzendorf. We should also mention the kindred movements of English Puritanism and Evangelicalism represented by such figures as Richard Baxter, John Owen, John Bunyan, John Wesley, and George Whitefield. The American theologian Jonathan Edwards represents the synthesis of all three movements. In this discussion Pietism will be used in the broad sense to include all these movements.

The Pietist emphasis was upon a holiness lived out in the world. The hope of the Christian is for eternity, but it is in this life that we are called to work out our salvation. There was among the evangelical revivalists an earnest desire for sanctification (*Heiligungernst*). Devotional literature (*Erbauungsliteratur*) including hymnology began to flourish. Chastity and simplicity were stressed, but celibacy was not regarded as the only path to chastity.

---

[3] See F. Ernest Stoeffler, *The Rise of Evangelical Pietism* (Leiden: Brill, 1965).

For the first time Christian marriage was seen in its rightful role as a partnership in kingdom service. The Christian family was looked upon as a little church or a church in miniature. A desire to bring the Gospel to the world outside the church was also characteristic of Pietist spirituality.

Out of the Pietist strand of seventeenth-century Protestantism various community movements emerged that were often of a monastic nature. Jean Labadie, a convert from Catholicism to Calvinism, established communities for single men and women in Holland and America. Jean Gennuvit, of Vennigen on the Ruhr (d. 1699), also attempted to restore the cloistered life. In the same century Johann Kelpius founded the Wissahickon hermitage near the present site of Fairmount Park, Philadelphia, in Pennsylvania. The piety of these communities was more mystical than evangelical, and the accent was placed on withdrawal from the world into the silence of meditation and contemplation. These experiments are to be associated with radical Pietism rather than the biblical Pietism of Spener and Francke.

In seventeenth-century England there arose the community of Little Gidding, founded by Nicholas Ferrar and comprised of members of the Ferrar family and relatives. Altogether the household numbered more than thirty persons. This community, which desired to work within the Anglican Church, saw itself as a middle way between Romanism and Puritanism. Nicholas Ferrar instituted a rule of daily devotion, but there were no monastic vows. Matins and evensong were said in the nearby church; the other canonical hours were said in the house. There was also a continuous prayer watch throughout the night. The piety of the community has been described by A. L. Maycock, a recent biographer of Nicholas Ferrar, as "biblical rather than sacramental." The members covenanted between themselves to live in a strict way, according to the Gospel of Christ. Nicholas' view of the Lord's Day was essentially Puritan: he desired it to be a day of rest rather than of pleasure. As he expressed it, the Lord's Day "frees us from bodily labours, but it should the more intend the exercises of the mind. God blessed the day and sanctified it; they must go together. If we would have it happy we must make it holy."[4] The community of Little Gidding functioned not only as a house of prayer and retreat but also as a school, dispensary, and infirmary for the surrounding district.

Community life became more prominent in Protestantism in the eighteenth century. We might mention here the community of the Pilgerhütte (Pilgrim's Cottage), founded under the influence of the German Reformed mystic and well-known hymn writer, Gerhard Tersteegen. Its members, who were all unmarried, bound themselves together in prayer, meditation, and labor in silence. From this community has come a rule that is regarded as a classic in evangelical monasticism.

Also worthy of mention is the Ephrata cloister between Reading and Lancaster, Pennsylvania, founded by Johann Conrad Beissal, a German Pietist who had immigrated to America. Like the Labadist and Kelpian groups, the members of this commune were millennialist and celibate. The colony was divided into three groups: the solitary brethren (unmarried men), the order of spiritual virgins, and married couples, who, on joining the community, pledged themselves to continence. The cloister supported itself by farming, fruit-growing, and such handicrafts as shoemaking, tailoring, and weaving cloth. It also operated saw, bark, and grist mills as well as a printing press. The members refused to take oaths and bear arms and for the most part eschewed all social and political involvement. Ephrata became noted for its music, which had an ethereal, mystical ring; several singing schools were established. The members adopted a

---

[4] In Gordon Stevens Wakefield, *Puritan Devotion* (London: Epworth, 1957), p. 58.

habit similar to that of the Capuchins and worked in alliance with the Seventh Day Baptists. The community, which at its height numbered three hundred persons, endured until 1905.

Most famous of all the evangelical communities in the eighteenth century was the Herrnhut community, founded by Count Nicolaus Ludwig von Zinzendorf near Berthelsdorf, Germany. This lighthouse, unlike Ephrata and Wissahickon, sought to work in close conjunction with the established church. From Herrnhut Moravian missionaries were sent to distant lands throughout the world; Eskimos, Hottentots, Red Indians, Kurds, Arabs, American Negroes, and many others were confronted with the message of salvation. In addition the community offered hospitality to refugees from persecution and other homeless people.

Although there was no general community of goods, the kind of sharing and intimacy prevailed that one would expect in a Christian family. The members were organized into "choirs" based on age, sex, and marital status, and these looked after their spiritual and material needs. There were dormitories for married couples, single men, and single women. According to their state (single, widowed, married), the sisters had their own distinctive ribbon, which they wore on their white straw hats; the brothers dressed simply in grey or brown. An hourly intercession for the work of mission was maintained around the clock.

The spirituality of Herrnhut was thoroughly evangelical, but the importance attached to the subjective experience of conversion and a felt assurance of salvation was foreign to orthodox Lutheranism. Hymn singing dominated the daily devotions of the community; the devotional texts, the *Losungen*, comprised the themes for these meetings. The trombone choirs of the community marked a new departure in Protestant church music. On Sundays there were preaching services as well as singing meetings. The piety of the community was anchored in the message of the cross, with a special emphasis on the "Lamb and Blood." Perhaps the main contribution of Zinzendorf was his stress upon fellowship as a means of grace in addition to the Word and sacraments. Other communal settlements founded by the Moravians include Marienborn, Herrnhag, Bethlehem, and Salem, the latter two being in America.

Mention should also be made of the Trevecka community of Howell Harris in Wales, which was a product of the evangelical awakening in that country. The community functioned somewhat like a Protestant monastery, although the members were not required to take vows of celibacy and poverty. In this experiment, which attracted about 120 people, the life of piety was integrated with the labor of the workaday world. The community remained within the Church of England, and its members went to the parish church in Talgarth for Communion.

The Methodist Circuit Riders, who traveled from one preaching station to the next in early American history, could be cited as an example of an evangelical religious order. Most of these men were celibate and lived in virtual poverty, although they were not organized in a religious community. Their celibacy was based on practical considerations and not an ascetic theological orientation. A man without family obligations was deemed more available for itinerant evangelism on the American frontier. It is well to note that Bishop Francis Asbury, the first Methodist bishop of this nation, embraced celibacy and highly recommended it to others.

The nineteenth century witnessed the proliferation of religious communities and missionary fellowships of a pietistic nature. Among the most notable missionary enterprises have been the Basel Mission, the Leipzig Evangelical Lutheran Mission, the China Inland Mission (now the Overseas Missionary Fellowship), the Wesleyan Methodist Mission Society, and the Sudan Interior Mission. What is significant about these missions is that they have given single people, particularly single women, the opportunity to serve full time in the life of the church. At the same time they give potent testimony to the fact that a married couple too, though not always having the mobility of their single colleagues, can be totally dedicated to the work of the Lord.

A mission station that came to function as a religious community was the Dohnaver Fellowship in South India, founded by Amy Carmichael who set out to India in 1895 sponsored by the Church of England Zenana Missionary Society and the Keswick Mission Committee. Earnest Christians from various countries and denominations joined in her work of evangelism and social service, the latter consisting mainly in reclaiming girls who had been sold into temple prostitution. Because of its increasingly interdenominational character the fellowship severed ties with the CEZMS and became a faith mission in which the members had "all things in common." Foreign and Indian personnel were truly "all one in Christ"; there were no distinctions based on rank, seniority or national background. Most of the members were single women, but there were also several married couples. A spirit of love and openness permeated the community, which caused E. Stanley Jones to remark: "If the kingdom of God has appeared anywhere on earth, it is here in Dohnaver."

An example of a community devoted mainly but not exclusively to the inner mission, that is, the evangelization of western Christendom, is the St. Chrischona Pilgrim Mission in Basel, which is still a vital enterprise. This lighthouse originally had as its aim the training of laymen or brothers who would serve as pastors in evangelical conventicles and mission stations primarily throughout Europe. In addition many Chrischona brothers have gone as missionaries to foreign lands. In 1909 a Bible school for girls was added, and in 1925 a deaconess house was founded. The girl who applies for admission to the diaconate must make two affirmations—that she has been saved and that she has a call. There are no promises

The Basel Mission

Dining Hall of the Deaconess House,
St. Chrischona Pilgrim Mission, near Basel

to celibacy and poverty, although it is understood that girls called to diaconal work will remain single. The few girls who go out as missionaries from the Bible school are known as mission sisters. St. Chrischona draws from Lutheran and Reformed as well as free churches.

Inner-mission work is likewise the main purpose of the Church Army, a communal-type evangelical order in the Anglican Church. This fellowship, founded in 1882, is solidly evangelical and is comprised of single and married men called "captains" as well as single women called "sisters"; married women may also have a part in the Church Army, but they are not known as sisters. The fellowship seeks to hold in balance evangelism and social service. Captains and sisters promise to serve for three years in the single state, after which they can get married or leave the order. Those who work in parishes assume the role more of a curate than of a deacon or deaconess. Their work is often of a practical nature, but evangelism is always their main concern. None of the officers is ordained except the working head, the Chief Secretary. Members of the Church Army have been active in both the Billy Graham crusades and the Keswick conventions. In 1912 a Church Army was started in the Church of Denmark in order to reclaim the urban masses for Christ. Church Armies have also been established in Australia, New Zealand, Canada, and the United States.

Better known is the Salvation Army, a kindred movement seeking to unite evangelism and social service. Unlike the Church Army it has chosen to work outside the established churches, although this was not its original intention. The Salvation Army can be thought of as an evangelical church rather than a religious order or community, though it is to be noted that in the Scandinavian countries Salvationists usually hold membership in the state church as well, even partaking of the sacraments in those churches on occasion. The Salvation Army makes a particular place for the single woman who desires to devote all her time and energy to the service of the church. The married woman, too, is given recognition as a co-minister in the church along with her husband. Much of the crusading spirit that characterized the Salvation Army in the nineteenth century is most evident today in the Jesus revolution and in vital missionary movements like Operation Mobilization.

The deaconess communities that emerged in the nineteenth century are another product of the Pietistic awakenings, although a few of them have also been influenced by the high-church or catholic movements within Lutheranism and Reformed Christianity. The emphasis in these communities has been primarily on *diakonia* or service rather than *latria* (worship) and evangelism, yet the latter are not wholly disregarded. Pastor Vermeil, one of the founders of the deaconess movement in the Reformed Church in France, has put it this way: "What was called for were souls entirely consecrated to their Lord, detached from themselves, and at God's disposal—souls whose solitary ambition would be to live completely by the Gospel, putting it into practice in the sight of men, and to preach by example and activity rather than by word."[5] In 1862 the Kaiserswerth Alliance was formed, which embraced the majority of deaconess institutions in western Europe; the most famous of these are Bethel in Bielefeld, Germany; Kaiserswerth in Düsseldorf; and Neuendettelsau in Bavaria. The deaconess movement penetrated not only Lutheran, Reformed, and Anglican churches but also Methodist, Evangelical United Brethren (*Evangelische Gemeinschaft*), Baptist, and other free churches.

In England, among the Anglicans, Methodists, and Presbyterians the deaconess vocation is generally understood as an ordination to church service rather than as a consecration to community life. Even so, the deaconess community of St. Andrew in London provides the opportunity for young women in the Church of England

[5] Biot, *op. cit.*, p. 75.

to serve as deaconesses in a community setting. In the Lutheran Church in Finland community life in a Mother House is still available for young women, but most of the younger deaconesses are choosing to work in a parish.

Communities of deacons have also been organized, although most of the deacons marry. Johann Heinrich Wichern, founder of the Inner Mission, was a guiding spirit behind the deacons. Pastor Friedrich von Bodelschwingh was instrumental in founding communities of deaconesses and deacons at Bethel in Bielefeld, Germany.[6] The brothers of Bethel promise only obedience, not celibacy and poverty.

The nineteenth century also witnessed a catholic revival within the Anglican Church and to a lesser extent within the Lutheran churches and the German Reformed Church in America. In the Church of England religious communities arose bent on the restoration of catholic ideals and practices. Among these orders with an Anglo-Catholic orientation are the Society of the Sacred Mission at Kelham, the Society of St. John the Evangelist at Oxford, the Community of the Resurrection at Mirfield, and the Community of St. Mary the Virgin at Wantage.[7] Their goal has generally been to adore God through liturgy and prayer, but they have also been concerned with equipping young men or women for Christian mission. The Cowley Fathers (Society of St. John the Evangelist) see as their vocation "to seek that sanctification to which God in His Mercy calls us, and in so doing to seek, as far as God may permit, to be instrumental in bringing others to be partakers of the same sanctification."[8] For the most part the spirituality of these

---

[6] Margaret Bradfield, ed. and trans. *The Good Samaritan: The Life and Work of Friedrich von Bodelschwingh* (London: Marshall, Morgan and Scott, 1961).

[7] The Anglican Franciscan community at Cerne Abbas stresses the active as well as the contemplative life, but its basic source of inspiration is also Anglo-Catholicism.

[8] Peter Anson, *The Call of the Cloister* (London: S.P.C.K., 1956), p. 79.

communities is mystical and even Platonic rather than biblical and evangelical. The Protestant Reformation is viewed as a divergence from the catholic tradition rather than the recovery of this tradition. At the same time there is in these communities an emphasis on mission and social service that is not found in a purely otherworldly spirituality, and the New Testament evangel can still be discerned amid their ceremonialism and rigorism.

Finally mention should be made of the utopian communities of the nineteenth and early twentieth centuries, many of which have their source in radical Pietism.[9] The Shakers, whose origins go back to the eighteenth century, are probably the best known of these in America. With their emphasis on new revelations and the deficiency in the material side of existence, they stand in the theological traditions of Montanism and Gnosticism. Living in agricultural communistic communities, they adhered to a God with both fatherly and motherly characteristics. They also had two messiahs— Jesus Christ, and their founder, Mother Ann Lee. Another evidence of their unorthodoxy can be seen in their attempt to communicate with the spirits of the departed.

Though men and women had separate sleeping quarters and abstained from sexual intercourse, they looked after one another and often engaged in spiritual conversations together. They also ate together in a common dining room though at separate tables. The two sexes even participated in the community dance together, though they were not allowed to touch one another. The dance was seen as a spiritual act and generally involved ecstatic shaking. The Shakers ideally did not seek to suppress but to spiritualize the bodily or physical emotions.

By the middle of the nineteenth century over four thousand people were living the communal, celibate life

---

[9] See Everett Webber, *Escape to Utopia* (N.Y.: Hastings House, 1959).

in fifty-eight Shaker villages. Shakerism has continued into the twentieth century but with declining spiritual fervor. Thirteen members of the Shaker community still live in Maine and New Hampshire. The sect was noted for its works of charity, ministering to illegitimate children, orphans, and homeless men. The Shakers also set high standards in agriculture, crafts, and furniture manufacturing. The contribution of the Shaker communities has been appreciated by scholars from such diverse backgrounds as Thomas Merton, Herbert Richardson, and Marcus Bach.[10]

Another nineteenth-century communal experiment was the Harmony Society, founded by "Father" George Rapp, a native of Württemberg, Germany, who advocated both celibacy and communism and won many converts from the established Lutheran Church. The Rappites came to America in 1803 and settled on five thousand acres north of Pittsburgh. In a few years there were a hundred houses in the settlement. In 1807 the community was shaken by a religious revival, and celibacy came to prevail thereafter. Because the land in Pennsylvania lacked adequate water facilities and was ill-suited to vineyards, the colony moved to the Wabash valley in Indiana in 1815. With later arrivals from Germany the community now numbered seven hundred members. Unfriendly neighbors and disease prompted the Rappites to move back to Pennsylvania after selling their village to Robert Owen, an English socialist, who renamed it New Harmony. Because of schism and lack of new converts, the new settlement, Economy, was dissolved in 1906.

Still other utopian or perfectionist communities were the Bishop Hill colony in Illinois, founded by Swedish devotionalists; the Amana community in Iowa; Brook Farm in West Roxbury, Massachusetts; the Aurora-Bethel

[10] See Thomas Merton, *Mystics and Zen Masters* (N.Y.: Farrar, Straus and Giroux, 1967), pp. 193, 202; Marcus Bach, *Strange Sects and Curious Cults* (N.Y.: Dodd, Mead, 1961), pp. 202-216; and Herbert W. Richardson, *Nun, Witch, Playmate* (N.Y.: Harper, 1971), pp. 129-131.

communities; the Society of Separatists at Zoar in Ohio;
the Jemimakins; the Adonia Shomo, a sect that grew out
of the Millerite revival; the Icarians; and the Oneida
community. Most of these were open to married as well
as single people, but celibacy became the rule among the
members of Bishop Hill and the Jemimakins (as with the
Rappites). The Icarians, Brook Farm, and New Harmony

Father Arthur Kreinheder, St. Augustine's House,
Oxford, Michigan

had their origin in the philosophy of the Enlightenment.

While many of these societies were characterized by a desire to build a this-worldly utopia that would emerge out of the dissolution of modern civilization, others were content simply to wait for the second coming of Christ. The strategy of all these communal ventures tended to be what H. Richard Niebuhr calls "Christ against culture" as over against "Christ transforming culture" or "Christ above culture."[11]

[11] See H. Richard Niebuhr, *Christ and Culture* (N.Y.: Harper, 1951).

5

The Community Revival in Europe

Since the period of the Second World War Protestantism has experienced a remarkable revival of community life.[1] What seems to distinguish these new ventures from the utopian and sectarian communities of the nineteenth century is that for the most part they seek to work within the established church and with the intention of serving both the universal church and the world. They often view themselves as orders or special working fellowships within the established churches rather than realizations or perfect embodiments of the kingdom of God. Most of these new communities have emerged out of a war-torn Europe, and many have been inspired by the vision of Christian unity.

Perhaps the best known of all the new ventures is Taizé, a Protestant monastery in Burgundy, France, that seeks to instill new life into the churches of the Reformation. It also is pioneering in the area of ecumenism; places of worship are provided for both Roman Catholics and Eastern Orthodox in the community's Church of Reconciliation. Taizé now numbers over seventy brothers, who come out of Reformed, Lutheran, and free churches. Some of the brothers live outside the community and work in parishes or have secular jobs, thereby carrying the presence of Christ into the world.

[1] See Donald G. Bloesch, *Centers of Christian Renewal* (Philadelphia: United Church, 1964); Olive Wyon, *Living Springs* (Philadelphia: Westminster, 1963).

For the liturgical offices and the Sunday worship service the brothers put on white liturgical robes; otherwise they wear ordinary clothes. When a brother becomes a full member of the community he must pledge himself to celibacy, community of property, and the acceptance of the authority of the community; these three vows or "engagements," as they are called, are meant to be for life. Solid theological writing is emanating from Taizé; both Roger Schutz, the prior, and Brother Max Thurian through their many published writings are becoming known as perceptive theologians.

Taizé presently attracts visitors from all over the world, including many young people, outside as well as inside the church. A recent conference on youth at the community drew eight thousand young people from forty countries. When the community church could not hold the crowd, the front wall was knocked out, and a vast tent was added. A subsequent conference during an Easter weekend drew eighteen thousand from over ninety countries for prayer and small group sharing.

The community also sponsors retreats and study sessions at its conference center at Cormatin, two miles from the monastery. Out of these "Cormatin Encounters" have grown conferences for married people called "Households of Unity" where the participants are encouraged to examine their vocation to marriage and their role as married couples in the work of Christian unity.

Taizé sees its overriding purpose as the reconciliation of separated Christians and indeed of all people who are now at enmity with one another. Outside its great church on the heights above the château are these words in four languages: "All who enter here be reconciled: father with son; husband with wife; believer with unbeliever; the Christian with his separated brother." The brotherhood especially strives for Christian unity, seeking to overcome the barriers that have for so long divided the Reformation and Catholic churches. Roman Catholic Franciscan brothers and a few Greek Orthodox monks have moved into

Church of Reconciliation, Taizé community, France

The Crypt, Church of Reconciliation, Taize

the village to lend their symbolic support to this amazing experiment in Christian brotherhood. Members of the community are often sent to live among the very poor in various countries of the world, where they bring the spirit of reconciliation to bear on social conflicts.

The community of Taizé has always maintained lukewarm relations with the Reformed churches, though lately there is a better spirit. Some Reformed pastors have accused the community of sacrificing truth to love in its openness to Roman Catholic concerns and values. It is commonly said—and not without some justification—that the Eucharist is given more prominence than the Word in the Sunday service, though the brothers ideally seek to hold Word and sacrament in balance. On the

Evening prayers at Taizé

other hand, some Roman Catholic conservatives were chagrined when the brothers gave financial aid to Pentecostals in Chile. Lately some Catholic radicals have sought to use the community as a forum to attack the hierarchy, but the prior has refused to grant their requests.

The fame of Taizé has brought with it certain penalties. Besides the continuing flow of visitors, there is now a public restaurant, a hostel for young people, and a huge parking lot. In order to preserve the integrity of the community the brothers have had to withdraw more rigidly into the confines of the château grounds. The community has always had its fulcrum in its daily offices, and if its worship were to be undermined, its very life would be in danger.

Near Neuchâtel, Switzerland, is the sisterhood of Grandchamp, which is closely associated with Taizé;

Community of Grandchamp, Switzerland

Chapel, Community of Grandchamp
A sister of Grandchamp

altogether there are about fifty sisters drawn mainly from Reformed churches. Their purpose is the service of God in worship and fellowship. While conducting retreats for individuals and groups, they do not see their role so much as the saving of souls as in helping people on their spiritual pilgrimage. Like the brothers of Taizé they seek to witness by vicarious identification with the needs and sufferings of others. Celibacy is defended on the basis of the availability that it gives for service. The members of this sisterhood wear simple blue dresses; a ring on their left hand symbolizes their spiritual commitment. The present head, Sister Minke, a native of Holland, is a woman of much charm and theological insight.

Another new sisterhood worthy of mention is the Casteller Ring near Würzburg, founded in 1950. The original impetus came from the Nazi-outlawed Bavarian Christian Girl Scouts, who dedicated themselves to bringing Christ to young women. Its base of operations is a castle on the Schwanberg, a mountain overlooking the Main river valley. The community is composed of thirty-five sisters who live a common life under a monastic rule. Being mainly teachers by profession, they seek to prepare young girls for work in social service. Though they wear ordinary clothes in their daily work, they put on simple black robes with white collars and caps for the four prayer offices in the community chapel. Observers can detect a spirit of happiness and openness among the sisters.

The Casteller Ring has been greatly influenced by the liturgical revival in the Bavarian Lutheran Church, beginning in the nineteenth century under Wilhelm Löhe. Communion is celebrated every Sunday; private confession and absolution are also practiced. The community life is directed by the prioress, Maria Pfister, and Pastor Johann Halkenhäuser, a resident chaplain. Adhering to the Benedictine motto "pray and work" (*ora et labora*), they see the Christian life as a joy and adventure rather than a "vale of tears" (as in much traditional spirituality).

Communities that have similarly been influenced by the liturgical awakening are Imshausen and the Order of Peace, both in West Germany. The former originated as a hostel for refugee children. It is now a monastic community of renewal, composed of both men and women who are endeavoring to overcome the barriers that separate Christians not only from one another but also from Jews and Moslems. The community recites the Divine Office seven times a day, starting with matins at 6 a.m. and ending with compline in the community chapel, which was once the cellar of one of their houses. The members of the Order of Peace, a communal fellowship of single women in Hamburg, Germany, seek to bear witness to Christ in their respective professions. Retaining some of the liturgical offices, they have a warm fraternal relationship with both Imshausen and Grandchamp.

The Brotherhood of Christ (*Christus Bruderschaft*) was founded by Pastor Walter Hümmer and his wife in

The Brotherhood of Christ,
Selbitz, W. Germany

The Chapel,
above, and
a procession, Brotherhood of Christ

Selbitz, Germany, as a center for spiritual growth and renewal. Having its roots in a spiritual awakening among young people in a parish that the Hümmers had served, the brotherhood is avowedly evangelistic without being sectarian. It functions as a double cloister with an equal emphasis upon worship, evangelism, and service. Besides the motherhouse there is a well-furnished guest house where the needs of the spirit are given special attention; a third house is now under construction for the infirm and old. The Brotherhood of Christ is composed of a hundred sisters and fourteen brothers who live in simplicity and celibacy, though there are no formal vows. Some of the members are engaged in nursing and parish and missionary work. The community works closely with the Lutheran Church in Bavaria and holds its Sunday worship with the parish church in Selbitz. With the death of Walter Hümmer in 1972 his wife Hanna has assumed the burden of leadership in the community.

In Darmstadt, Germany, is the Evangelical Sisterhood of Mary (*Marienschwestern*), a Protestant convent, which was founded by Klara Schlink, sister of Lutheran theologian Edmund Schlink, and Erika Maddaus with the support and guidance of Paul Riedinger, a German Methodist minister. The accent in this community is on intercessory prayer, Bible study, and evangelism. Born out of a revival in a Bible fellowship at the end of the Second World War, a revival characterized by intense conviction of sin and a desire to make reparations for the guilt of their nation against the Jews, the Sisters of Mary stress lifelong repentance as the gateway to eternal salvation. Klara Schlink, who assumed the name of "Mother Basilea," and her teacher companion in the Bible fellowship, Erika Maddaus, who became "Mother Martyria," are the two mothers of the community; the former has become noted for her gifts of prophecy and wisdom. An effort is made to communicate the Gospel not only by tracts and personal witnessing but also by drama; the plays of Mother Basilea are given in the "Call of Jesus"

Chapel of The Call of Jesus,
Evangelical Sisterhood of Mary,
Darmstadt, W. Germany

chapel and attract many thousands of spectators. The sisters provide for over five thousand guests annually, many of whom come for spiritual refreshment and retreat.

From its inception the Sisterhood of Mary has experienced steady growth. Its membership now exceeds one hundred; in addition there is an order of tertiaries called the Thorn or Crown of Thorn Sisters, some of whom live in a house of their own in the land of "Canaan" adjacent to the convent. There is also a small group of Franciscan Brothers who likewise reside in "Canaan" and who participate in the wider mission of the community. Daughter houses have been established in Israel, England and the U.S.A. The Sisterhood of Mary, like the Brotherhood of Christ, mirrors a spirituality that is closer to evangelical Pietism than to orthodox Lutheranism.

The *Marienschwestern* have had a difficult time in overcoming the fears and reservations of conservative Lutherans regarding monasticism. They have also been suspect because of their zeal in witnessing as well as their openness to the charismatic gifts of the Spirit. Some of their critics have accused them of religious enthusiasm (*Schwärmerei*). There is no question that the spiritual affinities of the sisterhood lie with revivalistic evangelicalism and not with confessional orthodoxy, whether this be Lutheran or Reformed. At the same time there has been some opposition to the experiment on the part of the Pietists and the sects, motivated partly by anti-Romanism. The sisterhood has maintained fairly good relations with the charismatic movement, though Mother Basilea has spoken out against the perfectionism that seems endemic to this movement.

While originally very open to the ecumenical movement, the Sisters of Mary now view it with suspicion because of its alleged liberal tendencies. Interestingly enough, their original name was the "Ecumenical Sisterhood of Mary," but Mother Basilea soon saw that the term "Evangelical" was much more appropriate. The community has won support from such church luminaries as Martin Niemoeller and Walter Luthi, though the latter has been uneasy with what he terms the "crude literalism" in Mother Basilea's book *The End Is Near*.

Some observers have also complained of the dictatorial policies of Mother Basilea. It must be acknowledged that a few women have left the order because of its seeming lack of opportunity for democratic participation in decision-making. At the same time it is an open question whether a community such as this that clearly goes against the stream could survive in its early years without a strong helmsman in charge. It is a mistake to contend that Mother Basilea is adulated or venerated by the sisters. They have the highest regard for her as one of the mothers of their spiritual family, but it is incontrovertible that their deepest loyalties are to their Savior, Jesus Christ.

Protestant Franciscan Brother, Darmstadt, W. Germany

Mother Basilea (left) and Martyria (right)
with some of the Sisters of Mary

Another relatively new evangelical community worthy of mention is L'Abri Fellowship in Huémoz, Switzerland. It was founded by Dr. Francis Schaeffer and his wife as a center for mission and witness to the disenchanted younger generation, particularly youthful intellectuals who have departed from the faith of their fathers. Previously Schaeffer, who had come to Europe from America after serving a Covenant Presbyterian church in St. Louis, spent a number of years as pastor of a small evangelical church in the Italian part of Switzerland. Besides the chalet occupied by the Francis Schaeffer family, there are five others belonging to the center, which can accommodate about 110 guests. The community is English-speaking, partly because of its many guests and visitors from other countries.

People come to L'Abri from all walks of life. The permanent staff numbers from fifteen to twenty. People are confronted with the Gospel both directly by means of worship and personal witnessing and indirectly by means of presentations and discussions exposing modern pagan philosophy, lectures giving the Christian viewpoint on contemporary art and significant books, by prayer, and by lives of sacrificial service. The spirit of love definitely permeates this community as searching questions by students are treated with respect and given honest answers. Any person may come for ten days free as a visitor; a Farel House student is charged $3.00 a day for three months. Each person is expected to study four hours every day and work another four hours. L'Abri is founded on the belief that life's categories should be integrated and that the Christian view of life and the world is a viable alternative for modern man. Thousands of young people, including many drug addicts, have found a new freedom in Christ through the ministry of this dedicated fellowship. Ancillary houses have been established in England, Holland, Italy, and France.

A quite different orientation characterizes the Iona community, founded by Dr. George F. MacLeod, a

Scottish Presbyterian minister, who saw in the depression
years that the church was not ministering to the physical
and social needs of men and women. Resigning from his
parish in the middle 1930s, he gathered together ministers and laymen, craftsmen in stone and wood, for the
purpose of rebuilding the sixth-century abbey of Celtic
monasticism on the isle of Iona off the northwestern
coast of Scotland. Every summer the group worked and
prayed together on the island, thereby demonstrating the
integral connection between work and worship, piety and
politics, clergy and laity. So the Iona community was
born, consisting of clergy and laymen drawn from several
denominations who seek to put into practice the historic
Christian faith. The Abbey was completed in 1965 and
now receives as many as a thousand guests and retreatants
each year. A youth camp on the island, sponsored by the
community, attracts two thousand young people every
summer. They join the guests of the Abbey and tourists
in attending daily morning and evening worship in the
Abbey church.

A small resident community lives at the Abbey
throughout the year, but most of the members of the
fellowship live and work in their own vicinities though
they share a common spiritual discipline and donate 5
percent of their disposable income to a common fund.
Among the projects of the community on the mainland is
the Community House in Glasgow, which operates an
inexpensive eating place for the working people of that
district.

Symptomatic of the way in which Iona serves as a
center for mission in today's world are the circumstances
surrounding the donation of Jacques Lipchitz' impressive
statue "Descent of the Spirit" in the cloister of the
Abbey in 1959. An American donor offered to pay for
the purchase and installation of this statue, which is a
duplicate of that which stands in a restored American
cloister in New Harmony, Indiana. Lord MacLeod refused
the donation unless a similar amount was raised for the

community's work among the deprived youth in a slum area of Glasgow. The sum was obtained, and the statue was then accepted. So beauty, history, and ecumenical vision were joined to social action, thus typifying what has always been the stance of this community.

Conservative Presbyterians in the Scottish church have viewed Iona with reservations mainly because of their fear that a social-ethical philosophy would supplant the biblical Gospel as the focal point of attention. It must be acknowledged that a secular mystical spirituality can be discerned in the life of Iona, but the community also seeks to maintain continuity with the evangelical and Reformed tradition. Dr. MacLeod himself, who not long ago retired as administrative leader of the community, has sought to hold in balance supernatural reality and social relevance and concern.

Cloister Arches, Iona Abbey, Scotland

New communal experiments have also appeared in England. In Sussex, England, St. Julian's community, comprising single women, was brought into being for the purpose of providing a place of quiet and retreat for missionaries on furlough and other Christian workers. Founded by Florence Allshorn, who had served as an Anglican missionary in Uganda, it has attracted support from Roman Catholics, evangelicals, and even nonchurch people. It now functions as a spiritual sanatorium for those who seek a respite from the pressures of modern life. The community includes three houses and a farm, which provides the major source of income. A sister community has been established in Kenya.

St. Julian's is noted for its concern for the whole person. Rest for the body is provided by private rooms, good meals, and comfortable facilities; the guests are given breakfast in bed. A spacious library helps to meet the need for intellectual stimulation. Worship is celebrated mornings and evenings, though attendance is not required of guests. The morning worship is primarily a time of prayers for the community; in the evening worship is often in the order of Anglican evensong and includes prayers for those known to be in need.

Stress on Christian candor coupled with a sensitivity to the needs of others is what has characterized life at St. Julian's. The importance of speaking the truth in love was a constant refrain of Florence Allshorn. The tranquility of St. Julian's has been forged out of potential conflict by group- and self-discipline. It has been attained not by avoiding people but by facing squarely what people are. The members of the community seek to learn from psychology and group dynamics but see the spiritual dimension as primary. Persons who are on the verge of a mental breakdown are not accepted, for it is recognized that some problems are beyond the scope of the community, but persons coming from treatment are usually welcome as guests.

Though the number of guests continues to increase

(there are now over a thousand annually), the number of members is decreasing, and this presents a problem for the community. The membership has never been more than sixteen. Florence Allshorn gave charismatic leadership that probably cannot be duplicated, though her successors have shown themselves to be discerning and thoughtful persons. Yet unless more women are drawn to this kind of selfless service, the community may have to change its character and direction.

The Lee Abbey community in Devonshire, England, which includes both married and single people, seeks to reach the lost for Jesus Christ by means of "house parties," a form of fellowship evangelism. The house party consists of a week or more of scheduled fun grounded in Christian fellowship and worship. Begun in 1945, the community now has over seventy members. Like many of the other lighthouses described in this chapter, it does not view itself as a self-sustaining organi-

Lee Abbey, Devonshire, England

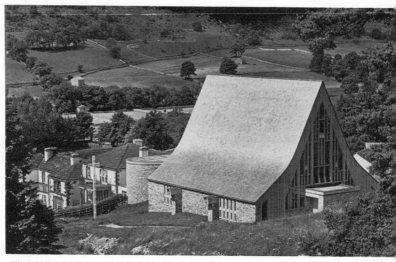

The Chapel, Scargill community,
England

zation separate from the church but rather as a "hand-maid of the church." Among the theologians of the community is Jack Winslow, an Anglican clergyman, who had formerly worked in a Christian ashram in India.

Similar to Lee Abbey is Scargill near Skipton in Yorkshire; most of its thirty members are single women, though there are some single men and two married couples. Its purpose is evangelism and Christian nurture. In the summer it sponsors house parties and in the winter conferences on various themes that relate church and world. It makes a special effort to forge bonds of reconciliation between Anglo-Catholics and evangelicals.

Operation Mobilization, founded by George Verwer, a graduate of the Moody Bible Institute in Chicago, is a young people's evangelistic crusade in which gospel teams are formed, mainly to sell Christian books and magazines containing the good news. The teams generally live together in community in groups of from ten to twenty. Besides distributing gospel literature they occasionally conduct open-air meetings. They usually try to work in cooperation with the churches in a given community. A few years ago a ship was purchased renamed *Logos,* which is used to carry Christian literature to various ports in Africa and Asia; at Lagos in Nigeria more than two thousand books were sold in one weekend.

At the central headquarters at Bromley in Kent, England, there is a community house occupied by four families and several single young men, another house for single men only, and a house for single women. A worship time as well as a study time comprise part of the spiritual discipline in OM. At the annual convention inspiring messages and rousing gospel songs give the youthful trainees purpose and direction before they set out on their missionary journeys.

The vision of Operation Mobilization was given to Verwer in 1958 while he was on an evangelistic mission in Mexico. He then saw the possibilities of dedicated Christian young people giving themselves to missionary work during their holidays with a minimum of organization. There are now gospel teams in twenty-five countries, mainly in southern Europe, northern Africa, and the Middle East. In some countries the members of the teams have been beaten and thrown into prison. Since the students live off the books and pamphlets that they sell, their life is characterized by austerity as well as adventure. There are five hundred full-time workers in OM, who enlist for a year at a time. The movement has attracted support from evangelical Anglicans, Plymouth Brethren, Pentecostals, Baptists, Lutherans, and various other Christian groups. Verwer comes from the Reformed Church in America, but in London he and his family attend the Assembly of the Brethren.

Though the gifts of the Spirit are accepted, not all are encouraged; the emphasis in Operation Mobilization is not on extraordinary gifts and uplifting experiences but on spiritual obedience and discipleship. The charismatic gift that is especially prized is helpfulness (Rom. 12:7), service beyond the call of duty.

A somewhat different emphasis is found in the Agape community, located on a lofty mountainside in the historic Waldensian valleys in northwestern Italy. Agape originally functioned as a work camp for young Christians after the Second World War, but in addition it now includes a community that was formally organized in 1954. Its purpose is to bear witness to the reconciling love of Christ in a world torn by dissension and hatred. It sees itself as an integral part of the Waldensian Church in Italy and also maintains cordial relations with the World Council of Churches. Unlike monastic orders it has no vows and a very free form of life. Its members support themselves and give generously to the upkeep of the community. In addition to sponsoring conferences and retreats it also functions as a house of hospitality where strangers and derelicts are made to feel genuinely welcome.

All was not easy in the early years of Agape. Sections

Agape community, Italy

of the Roman Catholic press in Italy accused it of being a "center of subtle and dangerous Protestant propaganda." Some of the traditionalists within the Waldensian Church regarded it with deep suspicion because it seemed to bear the earmarks of an incipient religious order. Agape calls itself a "community of service" instead of a religious order, partly in order to allay these fears but also because its life bears no resemblance to any kind of legalism or rigorism.

Tullio Vinay, a Waldensian pastor, was the first presiding officer or director of Agape and also one of the main theologians of the community. In the early 1960s, seeking to put into practice the ideals of Agape, he and his wife and several co-workers moved to Sicily to serve in Riesi, a small forgotten town located in a desolate section of that country. Out of what was originally a social service project has sprung the community of Riesi, which has brought new life to a dying town. Besides the preaching of the Gospel and the example of Christian

living, the community sponsors a kindergarten, a school
for mechanics, an embroidery workshop, and an agricultural school. Today twenty-four young men and
women live without salary at Servizio Christiano's "hill of
olives" outside Riesi. They eat simple communal meals,
work long hours, and worship together twice daily. Riesi,
like its mother community, Agape, receives solid support
from the Waldensian Church in Italy.

Other new communities in Europe that see themselves
as fellowships of concern and witness within the wider
church are the Christ-Bearers in Auerbach, Germany; the
Farncombe community in Surrey, England; the Sisters of
Pomeyrol in southern France; and the reorganized Brethren of the Common Life in Switzerland and Germany.
The latter includes a brotherhood, a sisterhood, and an

Chapel of the Christ-Bearers,
Auerbach, W. Germany

order for families. An independent branch of the Brethren of the Common Life has recently been established in Portsmouth, New Hampshire.

Also worthy of mention are these Lutheran monastic orders in Sweden: the Brotherhood of the Holy Cross; the Sisterhood of Mary Mother of Jesus; the Sisters of the Holy Ghost; and the Daughters of Mary, who also have a house in Denmark. The first is represented in America in the Congregation of the Servants of Christ, which has its center in St. Augustine's House near Oxford, Michigan. St. David's House near Rättvik in Sweden is not a religious community in the strict sense but a retreat house managed by a permanent staff including a Lutheran deaconess; five offices are observed daily at St. David's. The influence of Anglo-Catholicism can be detected in some of the Swedish orders.

Just as new communities are taking form, so many of the older communities are reexamining their mode of faith and practice in the light of Scripture and the new ecumenical climate. This is particularly true of the deaconess communities, which have been challenged to some degree by the new sisterhoods. The deaconess communities were originally founded for the purpose of prayer and service, but the pressures of church and culture have led many of them to minimize prayer and devotion. They are again seeing the need for spiritual life as well as social service. The deaconess sisterhood at Kaiserswerth, West Germany, is completing a house of stillness that can serve as a place of prayer and retreat. The Sisters of Reuilly in Paris are seeking to strengthen their community life and now have what corresponds to the three life vows. In 1956 the promise of celibacy was first introduced in that community. These sisters are also presently running missions in Algiers, Israel, and the Camerouns. The Sisters of Riehen near Basel are introducing evening prayers before bedtime in addition to the morning and evening worship services. There are also

*Member of the Brethren of the Common Life,
Stuttgart*

*Lutheran monk, St. David's Retreat House,
Rättvik, Sweden*

recommendations that married women be given a greater role in deaconess work. A diaconal year has been started in Germany and America in which girls give one year to serve in some deaconess institution. Surely this period of reexamination is very welcome, for it shows that the deaconess sisterhoods of our day are open to the renewing work of the Spirit of God.[2]

[2] See Donald G. Bloesch, ed. *Servants of Christ: Deaconesses in Renewal* (Minneapolis: Bethany Fellowship, 1971).

6

New Experiments
in America and Asia

Though the community revival was much more evident in Europe than in America immediately following the Second World War, there has recently been a notable upsurge of community life in American Protestantism. Yet because of denominational rivalry and the lingering suspicion of Romanism in our churches, many of these new groups have been compelled to organize apart from the church.

Koinonia Farm in Americus, Georgia, is a community whose spiritual roots are in Anabaptist evangelicalism. Founded in 1950 by Clarence Jordan and Martin England as an experimental center in interracial brotherhood, the community was under psychological harassment and physical attack for a number of years by the aroused populace of the area. Bombings and fires could not close the embattled commune, though some of its members were frightened away. Clarence Jordan, who received his doctoral degree in the area of New Testament studies at Southern Baptist Seminary in Louisville, Kentucky, has become known for his "cottonpatch" versions of the Gospels. Shortly before his untimely death in 1969, the community changed its direction and reorganized as "Koinonia Partners" dedicated to alleviating the plight of the poor by providing low-income housing.[1]

---

[1] For the story of Koinonia Farm see Dallas Lee, *The Cotton Patch Evidence* (N.Y.: Harper, 1971).

Koinonia supports itself by selling peanuts, pecans, grapes, fruit cakes, and candy. The community also raises pigs, cattle, and other farm animals, which makes it more or less self-sufficient. Through its Fund for Humanity it has enabled poor families, both black and white, to live in homes built by its members on a twenty-year no-interest-payment basis.

With the influx of visitors and volunteers and the vigorous house-building project for displaced rural families, Koinonia has lately aroused new opposition. The ten-year-old son of one of the members was stopped on the nearby highway by a man who cursed him for living with "a bunch of nigger-loving communists." One of the single members was hit by a sharp object thrown from a

Members of the Koinonia Farm Fellowship and
Residents of Koinonia Village, Americus, Georgia

passing car and had to be hospitalized. In the very culturally conservative area in which Koinonia finds itself it was to be expected that white natives would regard the community with suspicion if not outright hostility. Some of the members have become involved in acts of war resistance such as tax refusal and noncooperation with the draft, and this too has strained relations with the local populace. What is unfortunate is that the churches in the area have generally opposed the Koinonia Farm experiment; the few clergymen who offered their support soon found themselves without jobs.

From its inception Koinonia Farm has tried to see the spiritual and secular in organic relationship. It was Clarence Jordan's goal to minister to the whole man, and this includes the political and economic side of man's life. At the same time, in the early years of the community he was led to oppose some of his co-workers whose

Noonday meal, Koinonia Fellowship

motivation was purely humanitarian. He declared: "Man is not just a belly in search of bread. He's a soul in search of God."[2] In his view "the physical materials of life are tools of the Kingdom—a trust from God." Whether Koinonia can maintain this spiritual vision is a matter of conjecture, but its current work on behalf of the poor is surely laudable on its own level.

Adhering somewhat more closely to the Anabaptist tradition is the Reba Place Fellowship in Evanston, Illinois. Reba Place was begun in 1957 by Dr. John Miller, a Mennonite minister and New Testament scholar. Like Koinonia Farm it includes both married and single people. It presently numbers thirty adult members; altogether one hundred people (counting children and guests) live in the nine community houses. Unlike the Ecumenical Institute, another communal center in the Chicago area (see pp. 93f.), Reba Place sees itself not as a religious order but as a local church, yet independent of any denominational affiliation. The community is active in the local council of churches, however, and maintains an ecumenical stance. It has drawn people of many different backgrounds, including Episcopal and Roman Catholic, but 60 percent of its membership comes from the Anabaptist-type churches. Most of the members work in society but give their earnings to the community. Recently there was a surplus of almost forty thousand dollars, which was contributed to needs outside the commune.

Reba Place strives to be a concrete embodiment of discipleship in the modern world. It seeks to unite worship, fellowship, and social action. Its Sunday morning services are centered not in the preaching and hearing of the Word but in instruction in the Christian life; biblical drama as well as personal sharing play a major role. The basement of one of the community houses has

---

[2] Clarence Jordan, *The Substance of Faith*. Ed. Dallas Lee (N.Y.: Association, 1972), p. 58.

been converted into a coffeehouse where dialogue is carried on with interested patrons. The fellowship has also become involved in Evanston politics, taking stands in a local school-board election as well as on the issue of low-income housing. Members have participated in civil rights and peace demonstrations as well as in draft counseling. In contrast to the camp of secular theology, however, Reba Place sees the Bible as its final norm for faith and practice and affirms not only the Lordship of Christ but also His resurrection and second coming. Dietrich Bonhoeffer as well as the theologians of the Radical Reformation in the sixteenth century have been its spiritual guides.

Near Bedford in southern Indiana is the fast-growing Padanaram community, whose piety bears the marks of both the Anabaptist and spiritualist-mystical traditions. Founded seven years ago by Daniel Wright, a nondenominational Christian minister, it is characterized by a pacifist witness and a puritanical life-style. Of its seventy-five members, two-thirds are single. Lumbering is the main industry, and plans are now being made for a furniture factory and a tool-and-die shop. The members vote and pay local, state, and federal taxes. The name of the commune is taken from Genesis 28:2, 3 where Isaac tells Jacob: "Arise, go to Padanaram. . . . God Almighty bless thee and make thee fruitful and multiply thee, that thou mayest be a multitude of people" (KJ). There is presently a waiting list of one hundred families, mostly young couples, seeking to join the commune.

This community has no formal worship, regarding its way of life as its worship. The Eucharist is interpreted spiritually: any deep spiritual fellowship is a holy communion. Like many of the utopian communities of the nineteenth century it is anti-church; one must give up his membership in the organized church when joining the commune. The final authority for faith is not the Bible, though this is used as an aid to devotion, but the Spirit of God within the soul. The need of man is for inner enlightenment, thereby again attesting the mystical strain in this fellowship. Jesus is accepted as a spiritual teacher, but not as the divine Savior from sin.

In stark contrast is the evangelically-oriented Bethany Fellowship in Minneapolis, Minnesota, which views itself as a training center for lay missionaries. Though it was founded as a congregation of concerned Christians (mainly Lutheran in background) dedicated to mission, it developed into a religious community with both single and married members. The permanent resident staff now numbers seventy-five; there are 140 in the Bible or missionary-training institute. In addition to supporting missionaries throughout the world, Bethany Fellowship sponsors three daughter communities in Brazil. As a means of self-support the community makes trailers and grills; it also operates a printing press and several book stores. Pastor Theodore Hegre, its founder and leader, is

Dining Room, Bethany Fellowship

noted for his spiritual acumen and for such spiritual charisms as preaching, leadership, teaching, and healing. Speaking in tongues is regarded as a gift not to be despised, though not everyone who is baptized with the Spirit is expected to practice it. Bethany Fellowship has maintained a lukewarm attitude toward the charismatic awakening, welcoming its emphasis on the Holy Spirit but cautioning against certain excesses.

The theological background of Bethany Fellowship is the evangelicalism associated with the Holiness movement; its chief spiritual guides besides the prophets and apostles are Luther, Wesley, and Charles Finney. Lutherans and Calvinists might well question the perfectionist dimension in this fellowship, but one should note that sinless perfection is not one of its tenets and that in its view even the sanctified Christian remains vulnerable to temptation.[3]

For much of its life the Koinonia Foundation in Baltimore, Maryland, was also oriented toward overseas service, having originally been set up as a training center to alleviate the plight of the impoverished peoples of the third world. Its aim has been to reach them for Christ's kingdom by sharing with them technical skills and promoting literacy. In the view of this fellowship practical service is the most potent means of evangelism, though the question remains whether moral and spiritual values rather than the biblical Gospel are being promulgated. Lately the emphasis of the community has been on the development of personal spiritual growth and experimental education. The piety of this pioneering fellowship includes elements of both mysticism and Protestant liberalism.

The Company of the Cross, an Anglican community in Selkirk, Manitoba, manages a school for boys and includes both married and single people; the community

[3] See Theodore Hegre, *The Cross and Sanctification* (Minneapolis: Bethany Fellowship, 1960); and also his "*The Will of God Your Sanctification*" (Minneapolis: Bethany Fellowship, 1961).

has a marked ecumenical orientation. There are three kinds of members—initiate, associate, and full members. The last must make annual promises before a bishop of the Anglican Church to observe the rules of the community, including daily Bible reading and prayer, regular attendance at chapel services, and sharing daily in a common meal. Christians of other communions as well as non-Christians may apply for associate membership. All members receive the same living allowance irrespective of the work they do. Their ultimate purpose is "to spread that new life which our Lord brought to the world."

Communities in this country whose main source of inspiration has been the charismatic awakening are Daystar and Camp Zion in Minnesota and Harmony Hill near Mercedes, Texas. All of these are members of the wider charismatic fellowship, "Daystar Ministries." The spirituality of the Daystar Ministries is otherworldly and separatistic; the institutional church is generally regarded as apostate. Prophecy, personal testimony, and free prayer have just as much importance as preaching in their services of worship; in these sessions a place is also given to tongues and their interpretation. Scriptural authority is acknowledged, but it is believed that writings today can also have their source in the inspiration of the Holy Spirit and thereby can be equally authoritative for the Christian. "Marriage in the Lord" is highly regarded, but voluntary celibacy is also accepted. Despite their sectarian bent, these communities manifest a spirit of openness and sharing that is rarely found in the churches.

Other communities influenced by the charismatic movement are Zion's Order in Mansfield, Missouri, known originally as the Sons of Levi, and the Bethesda Colony in Gladstone, Manitoba, also called the Fellowship of Believers. Both communities, which maintain warm fraternal bonds, are interdenominational, though Bethesda was originally a Hutterite venture. Zion's Order was founded in 1951 by Dr. Marl Kilgore, a minister in the Christian church; it now numbers forty adults and

Zion's Order, Mansfield, Missouri

thirty-six children living in twelve family units. The members often conduct revival meetings in the various churches of the area. Bethesda operates a Bible school and carries on a radio ministry in the West Indies. Both these fellowships are dedicated to the apostolic mission of winning souls for the kingdom of God. Both seek to cultivate a spirit of goodwill with the churches and do not require members to give up their church connections.

Noted for their fidelity to church tradition as well as their ecumenical openness are the communities of the Catholic Pentecostal movement, many of which include Protestant members. We can mention here the Holy Spirit Convent near Lima, Ohio; the Word of God community in Ann Arbor, Michigan; and the True House and People of Praise communities in South Bend, Indiana. The Ann Arbor and South Bend groups have covenants that bind the members together in an openness to the Spirit and in service to one another. The communities are divided into smaller structural units called households in which the members, though not necessarily living in the same house, gather together to eat, to pray twice daily, and to share in recreation. True House has thirty-eight members, mostly students from Notre Dame University, and People of Praise has thirty-five members.

The charismatic revival is also reflected in the Jesus people, though their emphasis is not on the spiritual gifts as such but on open-air preaching and evangelism. Healings, tongues, and exorcisms are also common, however, as earnest young Christians seek to re-create New Testament Christianity in a secular world. The crusades of the Jesus people often take them into ghetto neighborhoods laden with crime and poverty. Many new communal experiments are arising out of this movement, with such names as Abraham House, Shiloh House, the House of Acts, Virgil House, Beth Nimrah House, God's Love in Action, and Love Inn. Though not all "Jesus freaks" live in communes or "Christian houses," as they prefer to call them, community life is upheld by many of them as a potent means to recharge their spiritual batteries for work on the outside. As one of their leaders expressed it, "community living is just a means to conquer the world for Jesus."

In the Shiloh Houses in Oregon and other western states a strict routine governs the life of the members; the day begins at 4:30 a.m. and lasts till 11:00 p.m. Virtually all the members are young people, many of whom were addicted to alcohol and drugs before their conversions. Courtship is encouraged in the communities, but it is strictly regulated. Those wishing to be married must be engaged at least six months. The girls are required to wear maxi-dresses in order to avoid sexually charged situations. The colonies, which for the most part are agricultural, are becoming economically self-sustaining. Their fundamentalist orientation can be seen in the emphasis given to the imminent second coming of Christ.

Somewhat more militant are the Children of God, who run communal houses where youthful converts are nurtured and instructed. Founded by David ("Moses") Berg, an itinerant evangelist, toward the end of the 1960s, the group soon became known for its practice of interrupting church services, thereby reflecting their alienation from organized religion.

The Children of God are characterized by a strict pattern of life. New members must sign over all money and possessions. If they have come out of the hippie culture they are required to have their long locks cut to symbolize that the hippie has died and a Christian is born. Each convert is also given a new name, usually from the Old Testament. This communal order rejects the profit-making of the straight culture as well as the escapism of the drug culture; it also repudiates the hypocrisy of organized religion. There is no democracy among the Children; their colonies are run by "Officers of the Lord" who plan policy and make all the important decisions. A strict morality is practiced; marriage is permitted only within the group. The Children often travel in buses, preaching the Gospel and making converts. Though they have been accustomed to going to bakeries and restaurants to obtain surplus food, wherever possible they try to raise food of their own. Most members are in their late teens and early twenties; about one-third come from a nominally Catholic background. Their sectarian bent is evident in their belief that theirs is the only valid style of life for true disciples of Christ.

Some parents of the teenage members of the Children of God have threatened legal action against the movement on the grounds that their sons and daughters have become alienated from them. According to retired Navy Lt. Comdr. William Rambur, one of the disenchanted parents: "We're convinced they're victims of some form of mind manipulation or why else their sudden change of behavior, wanting to destroy our institutions, not knowing or wanting us?" Charges have been made that letters of parents have been censored or never delivered and also that the members are not allowed to visit their homes even on holidays. The sect denies that young people are

Children of God at the World Council in the Netherlands

coerced to remain in its colonies and has recently eased its restrictions on visits with families.

The Children of God were originally located mainly in the Far West and Texas, but they soon expanded into other states and Canada. They are presently moving their operations into Europe with Bromley, England, as their new headquarters. A significant number of their nearly two thousand members are now outside the States. Because "Moses" Berg sees America as doomed, the Children are encouraged to begin a trek to a new land.

Like many other Jesus groups the Bible Way in Idaho, Washington, and a few other western states acknowledges the gifts of the Spirit, but its emphasis is on the daily practice of Christianity. Known for its ministry to drug addicts, this fellowship also engages in visitation evangelism. Bible Way Incorporated, the central headquarters, is located in Richland, Washington. The two communal houses in Boise, Idaho, are Stone House and the Bible Way Girls' House; in the former live married couples and boys while the latter is occupied by young women. The members in this city sell peanut brittle as their one source of income. Founded only a few years ago, the movement now numbers from seven hundred to a thousand.

The theology of the Bible Way might be denominated a Unitarianism of the Spirit insofar as it sees God as the eternal Spirit who is everywhere present; Jesus, in whom the Spirit dwelt, is the Son of God. Restorationist and premillennial doctrines are also very much evident. Worship services, which include preaching, exhortation, singing, and personal testimonies, are held every evening; prayer meetings take place at the beginning of each day. The group is radically sectarian, since it regards Protestants as children of the harlot, whom it identifies with the Church of Rome. True believers are urged to come out of the institutional church. The orientation of the Bible Way can therefore be seen as separatistic and otherworldly. Interestingly enough, many of its fifty members in Boise were formerly Episcopalian. The Bible Way has also established centers in some other western states.

While some groups within the Jesus movement have veered in the direction of cultism (such as the Children of God), cults of a definitely pagan character have developed on the fringe of the movement. In Chicago (as well as in some other cities) members of the Process Church of the Final Judgment hold to the eventual reconciliation of Christ and Satan. It is said that Christ will be the final Judge, and Satan will be the Executioner. Wearing black capes in winter and grey uniforms in summer, the Process people zealously distribute literature in the downtown areas. Adorning their dress are a silver cross and goathead emblem, symbols of Jesus and Satan. Among their projects are circles for developing telepathy and meditation and a kitchen-clothing shop where they distribute food and clothing to the destitute. Needless to say, the Process people are not accepted by the more authentic Jesus followers. Though they manifest comparable zeal and appeal to similar needs, the Process cult could be regarded in part as a counter-movement to the Jesus revolution.

Because it speaks to the spiritual needs of so many young people today, the Jesus revolution cannot be dismissed as a fad, though it contains faddish elements. It can probably be legitimately criticized for lacking theological depth and for tending to separate religion from the wider concerns of social and political life, but it must be remembered that religious experience precedes theology and that this movement is still too young to have produced much deep theological reflection. Also the attitude of the Jesus people toward the religious establishment may sometimes appear too negative, but all prophetic movements have voiced concern about the spiritual coldness of institutional religion, and the church should be able to learn from their criticisms. It is well to note that a community like God's Love in Action on the north side of Chicago encourages its converts to join local churches, but this is exceptional.

A danger that confronts many of the Jesus groups is that the emphasis on subjective religious experience tends to overshadow the concern for a life of costly discipleship. Much is said about the joy of knowing Christ, but not enough attention is given to the suffering involved in bearing the cross. Some of the Jesus people need to be reminded that the evidence of a genuine faith lies not in charismatic gifts or extraordinary experiences but in the ongoing struggle of love. Though not all the Jesus groups are Pentecostal, they are all nonetheless experientially oriented. By becoming more deeply grounded in the evangelical catholic faith and more truly open to the mainstream of historical Christianity, the Jesus movement would be immensely helped, and this would mean that the churches too would be benefited.

Several of the recent communities have been influenced in varying degrees by secular or radical theology, which is now beginning to shape the life of many churches here and abroad. Among these are the Martin Luther King community in Milwaukee; the Corryneela community in northern Ireland; St. Francis House in

The Lord's Fish House, La Mesa, California, offers Bible study and support to struggling Christians

DECISION photo by Mark Eastman

Kansas City, Missouri; Castle community in Minneapolis; the Community House, a predominantly lay venture in London, comprised mainly of Methodists; the Emmaus community in New York; the Community of Pope John XXIII in Oklahoma City, the Community of the Agape near San Francisco; the Christian Faith-and-Life community in Austin, Texas; the Vineyard in Dallas, Texas; the Parishfield community outside Detroit, Michigan; and the Ecumenical Institute in Chicago.[4] These communities, most of which are open to married as well as single people, see their vocation as the creating of a new style of life for our secular era. Social reform and political action play a prominent role in this kind of spirituality. The arena of salvation is regarded as the secular revolution rather than the crisis of repentance and faith. Jesus Christ is generally upheld as the contagious model of human adulthood, the exemplar of the new humanity, and sometimes also as the incarnation of divine love. But little is said of the sacrifice of Christ on the cross and His resurrection from the grave. His atoning sacrifice on Calvary does not loom nearly so important as His life of self-giving service. Indeed, it seems that Christ is primarily either a prophet or servant figure rather than the Savior from sin, though in some of these communities this is more a matter of emphasis than a doctrinal principle.

Located in the inner city of Chicago, the Ecumenical Institute is especially vulnerable to the charge that historical Christianity has been supplanted by an existentialist or humanistic philosophy.[5] Founded by Joseph Mathews, a Methodist clergyman, as a center for training laymen and clergy in the philosophy and techniques of cultural revolution, it sees God and man as co-creators of

[4] Note that Parishfield has disbanded, and the Christian Faith-and-Life community has been in the process of reorganizing.

[5] See Arthur McNally, "Religion for a One-Story Universe," in *The Sign* (Jan. 1968), Vol. 47, No. 6, pp. 30-39; William Petersen and Robert Coote, "Mr. Jones, Meet the Ecumenical Institute" in *Eternity* (March, 1973), Vol. 24, No. 3, pp. 34ff.; and Harold Brown, "Plumbing the Abyss" in *Christianity Today* (Dec. 8, 1972), Vol. XVII, No. 5, pp. 46, 47.

a new social order. Adhering to the axiom that "all is good," the community holds that in social conflict any means is acceptable in the realizing of its mission. With an emphasis on an incarnate spirituality it seeks to revitalize the life of both the church and the wider society by recovering the depth dimension of existence. In its intensive study courses salvation is depicted as humanization and Christ is presented as the model of the new humanity. Though its philosophy is suspect from the point of view of Christian orthodoxy, the enthusiasm and dedication of its members merit admiration.

Persons seeking membership in the Ecumenical Institute are asked to undergo a novitiate of one year before they can be accepted as full-time members. The members pledge poverty, chastity (within marriage) and obedience; the obedience is not to one superior but to the community. At the present time there are a thousand adult members, over two hundred of these in the Chicago center. The other members live in "religious houses" that are daughter communities of the Ecumenical Institute. Altogether there are thirty-six of these in North America and fifteen overseas, mainly in Asia. Every member receives a stipend for his work on behalf of the cultural revolution; it is enough to live on but not enough for luxuries. A couple with children are, of course, given more than a single member. The Institute and its religious houses are self-supporting.

The Ecumenical Institute seeks to cultivate a secular style of religious life, and this has brought it into conflict with many theologically conservative churches. Though oriented more toward existentialism than political theology, the Institute's espousal of cultural and social revolution has given it a radical aura. There is a daily office every morning. On Sundays the Eucharist is celebrated with the evening meal. No sermon as such is given in this service, though sometimes there is a very short meditation, called an "articulation of the Word." Liturgical symbols are valued as aids in coming to self-understanding.

Noticeably more anchored in the historic Christian tradition is the Community of the Agape in the vicinity of San Francisco. Its religious house, St. Martin's Monastery, is dedicated to the memory of Martin Luther King. Including both men and women, the membership of the community is mainly though not exclusively Episcopalian. The members, who are known as brothers and sisters, are pledged to poverty, chastity, and obedience. The fact that they wear religious garb is another indication of the Anglo-Catholic orientation of the community. Yet in its dedication to social justice and to the ideal of holy worldliness, it also bears the imprint of the new theology. One member, Brother John, is in a federal penitentiary for draft evasion. The life of the community is divided between prayer, study, manual labor, and the apostolate. The members do not seek to become more religious but more authentically human, and this humanity is realized both in adoration to God and in ministry to the world.

A fellowship that combines evangelical devotion and a radical social witness is the Post-American community in the Chicago area. It was started by several students at Trinity Evangelical Divinity School in 1971 and now numbers 25, including several married couples. The composition of the community is ecumenical; among the affiliations represented are Presbyterian, Plymouth Brethren, Southern Baptist, Roman Catholic, Pentecostal, and Evangelical Free Church. Its name is derived from the newspaper it publishes, *The Post-American,* which highlights the glaring discrepancies between the American Way of Life and the simplicity of the Gospel. The two living groups that comprise the community worship together on Sunday mornings at the Y.M.C.A. in Evanston. The plans are to relocate in Chicago's Uptown and to minister to the lonely, the forlorn, and the destitute. In the words of one of the founders, Robert Sabbath: "The American family is spiritually bankrupt. We chose community life because it was a way of resisting some of the American social values based on security. We feel it is a lot more possible to be human in a community."

A word should also be said about the Christian ashrams in India, many of which are related to the Protestant churches. The ashrams are small communal fellowships comprised of single and/or married people, often gathered about a guru or teacher who gives instruction in the Christian life. The supreme guru of the Christian ashrams is, of course, Jesus Christ, but many of them (although not all) see the need for a spiritual father or superior as well. The Christian ashrams generally hold to the traditional Indian ideals of ahimsa (non-killing), nonviolence, yoga, vegetarianism, poverty, and renunciation, but they see these ideals in the light of salvation through the grace of Christ. They are not viewed as means of salvation but rather as aids in strengthening our relationship with Christ. The majority of the ashrams seek to combine the contemplative and active life, with a place given to evangelism and practical service as well as worship and prayer. Ashrams have sponsored not only Bible schools and retreats but also model farms, hospitals, orphanages, and cooperative stores. There are more than fifty Christian ashrams in India, Ceylon, and Nepal.

The United Christian Ashrams, long under the direction of the late Dr. E. Stanley Jones, veteran Methodist missionary and evangelist, signify a marked divergence from the ashram principle in that the emphasis is no longer on living in a permanent community but on people coming together for a short period of concentrated spiritual fellowship. The Sat Tal Ashram in India, founded by Dr. Jones, consists of a permanent group as well as a one-month fellowship-retreat in the summer. There are also plans for a permanent community in Israel, but for the most part the ashrams of "Brother Stanley," as he is

called, are oriented about a one-week or weekend pro-
gram of spiritual renewal that combines aspects of the
Indian ashrams and the old Methodist camp meetings.
The only guru is said to be Jesus Christ; a committee of
twelve runs the local ashrams, and a committee of seven
oversees the entire movement. The ashram is viewed as a
foreshadowing or anticipation of the kingdom of God;
the emphasis is upon mutual sharing, rededication, and
spiritual conversion. Although the United Christian
Ashrams are located throughout the world, they have had
their greatest success in the United States and Finland.

Christian communities are also emerging in other Asian
countries. Among these is Jesus Abbey in northeastern
Korea, founded in 1965 by the Rev. Archer Torrey,
Anglican priest-theologian. Jesus Abbey is a house primarily dedicated to intercessory prayer for revival in the
church of Korea. It is comprised of both married and
single people and includes Anglicans, other Protestants,
and Roman Catholics. An attempt is made to combine
liturgical and charismatic types of worship. Other activi-
ties that are expected to grow out of the primary one are
evangelism, retreats, conferences, and rural development.
As in other evangelical fellowships community life is seen
not as an end in itself but as a means to a higher end—the
advancement of the kingdom of God. Jesus Abbey has
been somewhat influenced by the charismatic revival, but
it eschews all sectarianism and seeks to relate to the
established Korean churches. A second house, the Priory
of St. John the Baptist, is presently being erected at
Kaljon.

While most of the communal experiments seek to work
within the wider church and give support to its ongoing
mission, an increasing number of such fellowships,
especially in the United States, see themselves as embody-
ing a higher life and purpose than do the churches. The
ever present temptation in vigorous movements of reform
and renewal is to become self-righteous and self-sufficient

and thereby immune from criticism by fellow-Christians. The hope of the church today as well as of the new centers of spiritual renewal is to establish a relationship of mutual trust and cooperation in the fulfillment of their common goal, the heralding of the coming kingdom of God.

7

Toward a New Form of Community Life

Many of the recently established communities of our time bear the marks of the new spirituality that has penetrated both Roman Catholicism and Protestantism. The goal in life is no longer to withdraw from the world in order to commune with God but rather to serve God in the world. The Christian mandate is to identify oneself with the needs and sufferings of the outcasts and afflicted. Dag Hammarskjöld reflected the new emphasis when he said that the path to holiness lies through the world of action. Communities such as Taizé view the world as their monastery and the secular city as the modern desert. Calvin's concept of the world as the theater of God's glory is again being appreciated by the new breed of theologians.

A major influence upon the new spirituality is Dietrich Bonhoeffer, the twentieth-century Christian martyr, who was instrumental in founding a Brothers' House in Pomerania, Germany, in the 1930s; this short-lived communal experiment functioned at least part of the time as an illegal seminary. Bonhoeffer described its purpose as being "not monastic seclusion, but intensive concentration for outgoing service."[1] He envisioned "a new kind of monasticism, which will have only one thing

---

[1] Quoted in Mary Bosanquet, *The Life and Death of Dietrich Bonhoeffer* (N.Y.: Harper, 1968), p. 156. For Bonhoeffer's views on evangelical community life see his *Life Together* (N.Y.: Harper, 1954).

in common with the old, a life lived without compromise according to the Sermon on the Mount in the following of Jesus."[2] According to Bonhoeffer, only by serving with the utmost compassion in the world, only by living wholly for the world does one become authentically human.

The new spirituality is not exempt from criticism. Both those who embrace the religious life and life in the world need to be aware of the complementary truth that the world is a place of conflict as well as service. In the Bible the world is depicted as being under the subjugation of the powers of darkness (Eph. 6:12; I Jn. 5:19). Jesus Christ came to expel the demons, but His victory is actualized only in the community of faith. The world is, therefore, the arena of Christian warfare, the realm where Christians battle against the powers and principalities. An evangelical community needs to take this into consideration if it is not to succumb to utopianism or perfectionism. Bonhoeffer's community of Brothers was on the front lines in the battle against the Nazis and the "German Christians," but many of those who now follow him have lost sight of the biblical truth that the Christian must be *against* as well as *for* the world. George MacLeod, founder of the Iona community, has given this timely word of admonition: "By all means say that the secular is the realm of God's activity and that He is in and through all things. But realize He has both let loose Satan there, for our disciplining, and Christ is also there for our salvation."[3]

It should be noted that the new spirituality understands the Christian mission in terms of discipleship and the imitation of Christ. The theologians of the Ecumenical Institute speak of the need for a new style of life that will be able to penetrate the enclave of secularism; in their view Christian preaching seems to fail in this area.

[2] Bosanquet, *op. cit.*, p. 150.
[3] See George MacLeod, "Nearing the Eleventh Hour," in *The Coracle* (Dec. 1966).

Evangelism is being reinterpreted to mean dialogue and even social action. According to the new spirituality the way to witness to the world is by "Christian presence" rather than preaching. This simply means being with and for people, ministering to their needs in outgoing love. Charles de Foucauld, founder of the Little Brothers of Jesus, anticipated the new emphasis when he contended that we must "*live* the Gospel before we preach it."

Yet a community that purports to be evangelical as well as catholic will also adore God in worship and prayer and proclaim the glad news of redemption. *Diakonia* (service) is indispensable for a Christian life, but we must recognize that it grows out of *leitourgia* (worship) and *kerygma* (proclamation). Indeed, our outgoing service must always be held in balance with the evangelical proclamation. An evangelical community will uphold both Christian presence and Christian preaching. It will envisage the evangelical proclamation as one of deed as well as word. And yet the deed is meaningless apart from the word just as the word remains barren and abstract apart from the deed. At the same time we assert against secular theology that no life, however holy, can bring to men the assurance of forgiveness. One can gain this assurance only through the preaching and hearing of the Word of God. This is why in evangelical spirituality the sermon is seen to be the primary means of grace. This is why evangelism has priority over social service and political action (cf. Acts 6:1-4). It should be noted that such fellowships as the Evangelical Sisterhood of Mary, L'Abri, Lee Abbey, the Jesus people, Bethany Fellowship, and Operation Mobilization assign a prominent role to evangelism.

It is well to call to mind that many of the early deaconesses were engaged in missionary and catechetical work, as well as social service.[4] This was particularly true

---

[4] Significantly some of those who were enrolled as deacons in the early church such as Stephen or Philip became noted for their missionary endeavor.

of those in the Byzantine church. Today in the Church of England deaconesses must be able to preach and lead meetings. Deaconesses and deacons are being most true to Scripture and to their own tradition when they see their basic vocation as apostolic rather than merely humanitarian.

Yet we must also remember that there is a diversity of gifts and ministries. We are not all called to preach nor even to give formal instruction in the faith. There must always be a place in the church for those who devote themselves primarily to such services as prayer, healing, works of mercy, and social action, to name but a few of the specialized ministries. Yet all of these ministries derive their power and purpose from the ministry of the Word, and this means that none must be practiced to the exclusion of the preaching and hearing of the Gospel.

A comparison of two Protestant sisterhoods brings to light the tension between the new spirituality, which might be called a kind of secular mysticism, and an evangelical spirituality. The Sisterhood of Grandchamp in Neuchâtel, Switzerland, is characterized by its stress upon silence, contemplation, and following the example of Christ in self-giving service. Like the brothers of Taizé, they do not hold to evangelism in the sense of seeking conversions. They see their vocation as praying, waiting, and serving (as in the Parable of the Prodigal Son). The Sisters of Mary, on the other hand, in Darmstadt, Germany, see their mission as going out to save the lost (as in the Parable of the Lost Sheep). Evangelistic tracts, gospel plaques, plays, and personal testimonies are all means by which the sisters seek to make known the good news. Surely there is room for both of these approaches, but we would insist that prayer and waiting as well as social involvement must serve the great commission of preaching and teaching. The danger arises when a doctrine of universal salvation becomes dominant, thereby subverting the very basis of mission.

The sacraments, too, are necessary to the life of the

church and to religious community life as well. If a community intends to be both evangelical and catholic, it will seek to center its life not only in the Gospel but also in the sacraments, particularly the Blessed Sacrament of Holy Communion. P. T. Forsyth, the noted English Congregationalist preacher and exponent of a catholic evangelical theology, rightly declared: "The Sacraments are the acted Word—variants of the preached Word. They are signs, but they are more than signs. They are the Word, the Gospel itself, visible, as in preaching the Word is audible."[5] To exalt the Word at the expense of the sacrament is to lapse into a barren rationalism. This is always the temptation in the circles of evangelical revivalism, though such evangelical communities as Lee Abbey, Scargill, the Brotherhood of Christ, and the Sisters of Mary have succeeded in maintaining the sacramental dimension in their worship.

The liturgical revival today has sought to recover sacramental worship, and this movement has influenced many of the new religious communities including Iona, Taizé, the Brotherhood of the Holy Cross, the Congregation of the Servants of Christ, Grandchamp, and Imshausen. Yet in some of these communities the Word is regarded as of secondary importance to the sacrament. The service of the Word is seen as preparatory to that of the sacrament. We would again do well to pay heed to Dr. Forsyth, who contended that "the grand and new testament was not a Sacrament, but the Gospel. The only true catholicism is the evangelical. Its supreme Sacrament is that of the Word."[6] And the Catholic Franciscan, Bernardino of Siena, advised: "If thou canst do only one of these two things, hear the Mass, or hear a sermon, thou shouldst rather leave the Mass than the preaching, for the reason herein expressed, that there is not so much risk to

[5] P. T. Forsyth, *The Church and the Sacraments* (London: Independent, 1947), p. 176.
[6] *Ibid.,* pp. 47, 48.

thy soul in not hearing the Mass as in not hearing the sermon."[7]

Nor can personal testimonies, prophecies, and group sharing ever be substitutes for the preaching and hearing of the Word of God. In some fellowships influenced by the charismatic revival or tending toward spiritualism, the spontaneous inspired utterance is valued above the expounding of Scripture. Subjective illumination is given priority over the written and proclaimed Word. This is the peril in all forms of spiritualism and mysticism, and catholic evangelicals will seek to guard against it.

There is a quest today in both Catholic and Protestant circles for a new form of community life, one that reflects the new spirituality and particularly the liturgical renaissance. The social revolution is also important in the minds of many who desire to make a meaningful and relevant witness. The new ideal is a fellowship that relates its worship to ongoing needs and concerns in the world. This ideal is irreproachable, but we believe that it needs deeper Scriptural undergirding if it is to penetrate the world of our time.

Whereas the old spirituality placed the accent on separation from the world and the new spirituality speaks of identification with the world, the spirituality we uphold stresses combat against the world. This indeed was the hallmark of Reformation theology as well as of the spiritual movements of purification subsequent to the Reformation, namely, Puritanism and Pietism. An evangelical community, like the wider evangelical church, will see itself neither as a cloistered fortress apart from society nor as one of the power structures of the society. Rather it will view itself as a vanguard in the army of the saints who are called to battle with a hostile world. We do not seek solidarity with the world but the conquest of the world for Jesus Christ. At the same time

[7] Quoted in Samuel M. Shoemaker, *By the Power of God* (N.Y.: Harper, 1954), p. 128.

it should be recognized that this warfare is spiritual, and our weapons are therefore spiritual; they include the preaching and hearing of the Gospel, praying, Bible study, and fasting. In this view, asceticism is not a method of salvation but training for mastery and combat. This is the evangelical spirituality so sorely needed today, and it is to be clearly distinguished from the Platonic mystical spirituality that has dominated much of Catholicism in the past as well as the secular spirituality of the new-breed theologians.

To some extent the spirituality that we advocate was realized in some earlier communities such as Herrnhut and Trevecka. It is also present in varying degrees in some of the new Protestant communities: the Brotherhood of Christ, L'Abri, Lee Abbey, the Sisters of Mary, and Operation Mobilization. Others, too, could be included. Such groups are symbols of separation as well as of identification. The separation is not from the needs of the world but from its sin. The identification is not with the spirit of the world but with its suffering.

An evangelical community will uphold the biblical ideal of holiness in the world. But this is also a holiness that is directed toward the world to come. The spirituality of such a community will be both this-worldly and otherworldly. Just as there is a false otherworldliness that disregards this world, so there is a true otherworldliness that gives significance to this world. The former is mystical and gnostic; the latter is biblical and evangelical. Our ultimate loyalty is to the holy God who stands over against this world, but we are called to exercise this loyalty in the midst of the grime and agony of this world.

It is interesting to note that the Bethlehem deaconess community at Hamburg follows a rule that affirms that the "life of the deaconess is led in the world, for the service of man, but it is at the same time the service of God. Now prayer is the principal service of God."[8] Here

[8] Biot, *The Rise of Protestant Monasticism*, p. 79.

we see how a community unites the old and new spiritualities, but at the same time gives priority to the glory of God.

An evangelical community will seek a balance between contemplation and action. We need to draw close to God in adoration, prayer, and meditation, but we must then return to the world spiritually empowered to serve our fellow man. Teresa of Avila is right that the church needs both Marys and Marthas, and that Martha may well be doing a more significant work at a particular time. What is important to recognize is that the highest service of the contemplative is listening to and pondering the Word of God; the highest service of the activist is proclaiming this Word to the world.

It can be said that one reason the church has so little impact upon modern culture is that it is too much in the culture. Before the church can penetrate the mind and soul of the culture, it needs to be immersed in the mind and soul of God. Secular and political theologians speak of the need for greater involvement in the life of the world, and yet it may be that the dire need of Christians today is for a more radical withdrawal from the world. Surely religious communities in our time can play an important role by providing Christians with an opportunity for retreat and withdrawal from the trivialities and pressures of ordinary life. Paul Tillich contends that ministers in particular need to withdraw from the pressures of modern society if they would remain relevant. He holds that

> in order to communicate the gospel we need nonparticipation. Ministers need withdrawal and retirement from those influences beating upon them every minute. This, perhaps, is the most difficult task. Ministers belong to those who participate, and have only weak weapons to resist this participation.[9]

[9] Paul Tillich, *Theology of Culture.* Ed. Robert C. Kimball (N.Y.: Oxford U.P., 1959), p. 206.

Karl Barth, probably the most brilliant expositor of evangelical theology in our time, has been noted for his sharp criticisms of monastic and mystical spirituality. Nevertheless he sees the need for a new form of community life, one that will reflect the evangelical message of the Reformation. He warns against those theologians who advocate involvement and participation in secular culture without at the same time sounding the call to retreat.

> Can there be either for the Church or for individuals any genuine approach to the world or man unless there is an equally genuine retreat? Has there not to be (not merely a healthy but a spiritually necessary) rhythm in this matter, in which there will always be a place for the $\dot{\alpha}\nu\alpha\chi\omega\rho\epsilon\hat{\iota}\nu$ [act of withdrawing]?[10]

One of the primary goals of an evangelical community is the changing of man's nature through the preaching of the Gospel. The regeneration of sinners is surely the principal means to the glorification of God. Yet communities, as well as churches, must also be concerned about improving man's material lot, since our ministry is to the whole man. William Booth, founder of the Salvation Army, had as his motto "soup, soap and salvation," but he never confused the soup and soap with salvation, which is the temptation of certain secular and radical theologians today. The point is that we must sometimes be Good Samaritans before we can be heralds. Yet service to our neighbor must always have for its goal his conversion to God, since this indeed is the greatest good that could happen to him. St. Teresa put it this way: "The soul of the care of the poor is the care of the poor soul."

When the church is no longer a center of light, when it is no longer a citadel of prayer, when it is no longer a powerhouse for evangelism, then there is a need for new

---

[10] Karl Barth, *Church Dogmatics.* Eds. G. W. Bromiley and T. F. Torrance (Edinburgh: T. and T. Clark, 1958), Vol. IV, Part 2, p. 14.

forms of Christian witness that can remind the world of
the claims of the Gospel. Christoph Blumhardt has rightly
said:

> God always wants to have a place, a community, which
> belongs to Him really and truly, so that God's being can
> dwell there. God needs such a place from where He can work
> for the rest of the world. There must be a place on the earth
> from where the sun of God's kingdom shines forth.[11]

Among the most significant lighthouses that have
arisen in protest against the worldliness of the church are
religious communities. Such ventures might be considered
para-parochial forms, since they exist alongside of the
parish or institutional church. At the same time it is
important that they be in organic relationship with the
church lest they become sectarian. According to Walter
Hümmer, co-founder of the Brotherhood of Christ,
without the community or brotherhood, parishes are in
danger of becoming mere social clubs; on the other hand,
without the parishes, a community is tempted to become
another sect. This latter danger is certainly present in
both the Padanaram community in Indiana and the
charismatic Daystar ministries in Minnesota and Texas. A
religious community should ideally be an *ecclesiola* (little
church) in the ecclesia.

At this point it is appropriate to consider the precise
nature or role of a biblically based community or
brotherhood in the world today. Such a brotherhood will
first of all be evangelical. That is to say, it will witness to
the biblical message of justification by free grace, the
message rediscovered by the Protestant Reformation. It
will uphold Jesus Christ as the Savior from sin and not
simply as the "man for others." Such a community will
be a congregation under the Word, one that draws its
principal source of inspiration from Holy Scripture.

---

[11] R. Lejeune, ed. *Christoph Blumhardt and His Message* (Woodcrest,
Rifton, N.Y.: Plough, 1963), p. 81.

Indeed, some of the new religious communities are of this very nature. This emphasis does not exclude Roman Catholic or Eastern Orthodox fellowships, for these, too, can be reformed in the light of the Gospel of free grace; in a few of these orders such a reform is already taking place. Such fellowships as the Moral Re-Armament community in Caux, Switzerland, and the Thomas Merton Center in Quebec, Canada, because of their tendency to syncretism and eclecticism, conflict with the evangelical ideal. A Roman Catholic fellowship like the Focalari, on the other hand, which is Bible centered and which witnesses to the life-changing power of faith, is much more in accord with New Testament Christianity.[12]

Again the new-style brotherhood will be a sign of the Christian community, the outgoing fellowship of love that is the church. Indeed, such a brotherhood will be the church in miniature, a small-scale model of the church. Although giving a central place to worship, it will also regard fellowship and service as highly important. It will remind the world that the church of Jesus Christ, the community of faith in the risen Savior, is a visible reality. In this time of impersonalization and dehumanization a religious community should seek to function not as a self-enclosed ecclesiastical order prone to rigorism and legalism but as a Christian family, where there is mutual sharing and respect for the opinions of others. This does not necessarily mean that every voice would have equal validity; indeed, in a family the authority of father and mother is still at least partially maintained. Being a model of corporate life, such a community will witness to the

[12] The Focalari, begun in 1943, have a core group of 1750 who live in community under the disciplines of poverty, chastity, and obedience and devote themselves to evangelization. In another category are over seven thousand people who witness to Christ in their secular vocations and serve the movement in their spare time. The Focalari, like Protestant evangelicals, make use of the testimonial, for they are eager to tell of the life-changing power of faith in their own lives.

truth that the fragmentation of modern life can be overcome.[13]

A mixed community, including both men and women, is probably a more potent sign of the church as the family of God than an exclusive community of sisters or brothers. We nonetheless also see the value of separate sisterhoods and brotherhoods in that they can probably maintain a higher level of discipline than the mixed community, particularly one with children. On the other hand, unless they continually maintain contact with the outside world, they are more likely to become ingrown and rigid.

Another distinguishing mark of an evangelical community is that it will be an agent of reconciliation between the churches. It will work to break down the barriers that divide the family of God, particularly those of a cultural and racial character. It will also seek to maintain continuity with the church tradition and therefore will be catholic as well as evangelical. At the same time it will not subordinate truth to love and will seek a united church only on the basis of fidelity to the Word of God declared in Holy Scripture.

A community that upholds Christ as Lord and Savior will also be outreaching. It will be imbued with an evangelistic missionary fervor to bring the Gospel of reconciliation and redemption to a spiritually lost world. One of the failings of much traditional cloistered piety was that the great commission to preach the Gospel to all peoples was often ignored. Prayer was rightly stressed, but neither prayer nor service is a substitute for preaching. We are not all called to be ministers of the Word and sacraments, but it is incumbent upon every believer to witness to Christ in word as well as deed. And every

---

[13] A local church congregation in which the spirit of brotherly love is very much manifest can also function as a sign of the eschatological family of God.

Christian must hear the Word proclaimed if he is to stand firm in the faith.

It is important to recognize, too, that an evangelical brotherhood or sisterhood will be in conflict with the dominant values and spirit of the culture. It will seek to be a beachhead of the kingdom of light in an alien and hostile world. Such a community can be regarded as an oasis of spiritual life in the modern desert of secularism and nihilism. Because of its radical witness to the Lordship and Saviorhood of Christ, the lines between the church and the world become very evident in this kind of community. It should be borne in mind that many of the new evangelical communities have suffered severe persecution not only from the world but also from vested interests within the church. In such a fellowship one can perceive the victory of Christ over the powers of darkness.

In this connection it should be noted that evangelical communities, like the churches from which they come, will usually retain the moral dualism of the New Testament faith, which sees the world as a battleground between God and Satan, faith and unbelief, righteousness and sin. This kind of dualism stands in contrast to a philosophical monism as well as to a metaphysical dualism, both of which pervade the mystical tradition. Instead of seeing all men and the whole world in the body of Christ, the biblical Christian sees the body of Christ as a colony of heaven in a world still largely under the domain of the powers of darkness. God, to be sure, is acknowledged as the power over the powers of the world, but though they have been dethroned by the cross and resurrection victory of Christ, God permits them to exercise their tyranny for a time.

Finally the new-style community will be an eschatological sign of the coming kingdom of God. It will bear a radical witness to the new aeon in which men will no longer be united by blood or race but solely by faith in

Jesus Christ. Father Biot has rightly said: "And precisely in order to be an eschatological sign, this original Christian life must be pursued in a kind of secession from the values of the temporal order: wealth, family, independence."[14] Religious communities have always borne witness to the ephemeral character of life by their utter simplicity and childlike obedience. What makes an evangelical community distinctive is that it will openly proclaim the coming again of Christ in power and glory in order to set up the kingdom that shall have no end. It will remind the world that we are living in the latter days and that the shadow of divine judgment looms on the horizon. Such a community will not only witness to the end by deed but also by word.

An evangelical catholic spirituality cannot be maintained apart from constant reexamination of the faith as well as continual reform in the organized life of the community. Our faith should be challenged as well as fortified if it is to mature and become strong. Piety must never neglect critical examination and rational inquiry. Neither a church nor a religious community desires robots but mature men and women who witness to the faith because they understand it and have personally appropriated it. An evangelical catholic community will therefore make room for study as well as prayer, for instruction as well as proclamation.

The church of Jesus Christ has always benefited from the radical ascetic protest, the example of revolutionary love, which serves as a prophetic reminder of the unconditional claims of the Gospel that are laid upon all those who would follow Jesus Christ. Community life is only one option, of course, for those who would be beacon lights of the Gospel today. Certainly we shall always need Christians who live in the very midst of society and witness to Christ in their secular vocations. A combination of these two patterns of discipleship can be

[14] Biot, *op. cit.*, p. 132.

seen in various communities (such as Taizé, Iona, Reba Place, and the Order of Peace) in which members often work in society while still belonging to the communal fellowship. Yet the option of detachment and separation from the hectic world of secular pursuits should also be open to earnest Christians. In this time of affluence, moral decay, and war prosperity, both the church and world stand in dire need of such a witness.

Bibliography

Allchin, A. M. *The Silent Rebellion*. London: SCM Press, 1958.

Allshorn, Florence. *The Notebooks of Florence Allshorn*. London: SCM Press, 1956.

Andrews, Edward. *The People Called Shakers*. New York: Dover Publications, 1963.

Anson, Peter. *The Call of the Cloister*. London: S.P.C.K., 1956.

Armytage, G. *Heavens Below: Utopian Experiments in England 1560-1960*. Toronto: University of Toronto Press, 1961.

Arnold, Emmy. *Torches Together: The Beginning and Early Years of Bruderhof Communities*. Woodcrest, Rifton, N.Y.: Plough Publishing House, 1971.

Bach, Marcus. *Strange Sects and Curious Cults*. New York: Dodd, Mead and Company, 1961.

Bestor, Arthur Eugene, Jr. *Backwoods Utopias*. Philadelphia: University of Pennsylvania Press, 1950.

Bettelheim, Bruno. *The Children of the Dream*. New York: The Macmillan Company, 1969.

Biot, Francois. *The Rise of Protestant Monasticism*. Translated by W. J. Kerrigan. Baltimore: Helicon Press, 1963.

Bisagno, John R. *The Jesus Revolution: New Inspiration for Evangelicals*. Nashville: Broadman Press, 1971.

Blessitt, Arthur. *Turned On to Jesus*. New York: Hawthorne Books, 1971.

Bloesch, Donald G. *Centers of Christian Renewal*. Philadelphia: United Church Press, 1964.

———. *The Reform of the Church*. Grand Rapids: Wm. B. Eerdmans Publishing Company, 1970.

———, editor. *Servants of Christ: Deaconesses in Renewal*. Minneapolis: Bethany Fellowship, 1971.

Bonhoeffer, Dietrich. *Life Together*. New York: Harper and Row, 1954.

Bradfield, Margaret, editor. *The Good Samaritan: The Life Story* of "Father" Bodelschwingh. London: Marshall, Morgan and Scott, 1961.

Carden, Maren Lockwood. *Oneida: Utopian Community to Modern Corporation.* New York: Harper and Row, 1971.

Chavchavadze, Marina, editor. *Man's Concern with Holiness.* London: Hodder and Stoughton, 1970.

Clark, Stephen B. *Building Christian Communities.* Notre Dame, Indiana: Ave Maria Press, 1972.

Coles, Robert. *A Spectacle Unto the World: The Catholic Worker Movement.* New York: Viking Press, 1973.

Conkin, Paul K. *Two Paths to Utopia: The Hutterites and the Llano Colony.* Lincoln: University of Nebraska Press, 1964.

Desroche, Henri. *The American Shakers: From Neo-Christianity to Presocialism.* Amherst: University of Massachusetts Press, 1971.

Drakeford, John W. *Children of Doom.* Nashville: Broadman, 1972.

Drolet, Francis. *New Communities for Christians.* Staten Island, New York: Alba House, 1972.

Durnbaugh, Donald F. *The Believers' Church: The History and Character of Radical Protestantism.* New York: The Macmillan Company, 1968.

Enroth, Ronald, *et al. The Jesus People: Old-Time Religion in the Age of Aquarius.* Grand Rapids: Wm. B. Eerdmans Publishing Company, 1972.

Ferguson, Charles W. *The New Books of Revelation.* New York: Doubleday, Doran and Company, 1928.

Fitzgerald, George R. *Communes: Their Goals, Hopes, Problems.* New York: Paulist Press, 1972.

Fogarty, Robert S. *American Utopianism.* Itasca, Ill.: F. E. Peacock Publishers, Inc., 1972.

Francis, Fr. *Brother Douglas.* London: A. R. Mowbray and Company, 1961.

Heasman, Kathleen. *Army of the Church.* London: Lutterworth Press, 1968.

Hedgepeth, William and Stock, Dennis. *The Alternative: Communal Life in New America.* New York: Macmillan, 1970.

Hegre, Theodore. *The Cross and Sanctification.* Minneapolis: Bethany Fellowship, 1960.

Hendricks, Robert J. *Bethel and Aurora.* N.Y.: Press of the Pioneers, 1933.

Hine, Robert. *California Utopian Communities.* New Haven: Yale University Press, 1966.

Holloway, Mark. *Heavens on Earth: Utopian Communities in America 1680-1880.* New York: Dover Publications, Inc., 1966.

Hostetler, John A. *Hutterite Life.* Scottdale, Penn.: Herald Press, 1965.

Houriet, Robert. *Getting Back Together.* New York: Coward, Mc-Cann and Geoghegan, 1972.

Jordan, Clarence. *The Substance of Faith.* New York: Association Press, 1972.

Jorstad, Erling. *That New-Time Religion: The Jesus Revival in America.* Minneapolis: Augsburg, 1972.

Kanter, Rosabeth Moss. *Commitment and Community.* Cambridge, Mass.: Harvard University Press, 1972.

Klein, Walter C. *Johann Conrad Beissal, Mystic and Martinet 1690-1768.* Philadelphia: University of Pennsylvania Press, 1942.

Kortzfleisch, Siegfried von. *Mitten Im Herzen Der Massen.* Stuttgart: Kreuz-Verlag, 1963.

Lee, Dallas. *The Cotton Patch Evidence.* New York: Harper and Row, 1971.

Leete, Frederick. *Christian Brotherhoods.* Cincinnati: Jennings and Graham, 1912.

Lewis, A. J. *Zinzendorf the Ecumenical Pioneer.* Philadelphia: Westminster Press, 1962.

Lubich, Chiara. *That All Men Be One: Origins and Life of the Focalare Movement.* New York: New City Press, 1969.

MacDonald, John A. *House of Acts.* Carol Stream, Ill.: Creation House, 1970.

MacLeod, George. *We Shall Rebuild.* Philadelphia: Kirkridge Press, 1945.

Mallott, Floyd E. *Studies in Brethren History.* Elgin, Ill.: Brethren Publishing House, 1954.

Maycock, Alan. *Chronicle of Little Gidding.* London: S.P.C.K., 1954.

McFadden, Michael. *The Jesus Revolution.* New York: Harper and Row, 1973.

Melcher, Marguerite Fellows. *The Shaker Adventure.* Princeton: Princeton University Press, 1941.

Merton, Thomas. *Mystics and Zen Masters.* New York: Farrar, Strauss and Giroux, 1967.

Miller, William D. *A Harsh and Dreadful Love: Dorothy Day and the Catholic Worker Movement.* New York: Liveright, 1973.

Modersohn, Ernst. *Men of Revival in Germany.* Frankfurt: Herold Publishers, n.d.

Moore, Peter C. *Tomorrow Is Too Late—The Story of Taizé.* New York: Morehouse-Barlow, 1972.

Moran, Gabriel. *The New Community.* New York: Herder and Herder, 1970.

Morton, Ralph. *Community of Faith.* New York: Association Press, 1954.

———. *The Iona Community Story.* London: Lutterworth Press, 1957.

Mottu, Philippe. *The Story of Caux: From La Belle Epoque to Moral Re-Armament.* Pinner, England: Grosvenor Books, 1970.

Muncy, Raymond Lee. *Sex and Marriage in Utopian Communities: 19th-century America.* Bloomington: Indiana University Press, 1973.

Nordhoff, Charles. *The Communistic Societies of the United States.* New York: Hilary House Publishers, Ltd., 1961.

Oldham, J. H. *Florence Allshorn and the Story of St. Julian's.* London: SCM Press, 1956.

Pederson, Duane. *Jesus People.* Cleveland: Regal, 1971.

Perchenet, A. *The Revival of the Religious Life and Christian Unity.* Translated by E. M. A. Graham. London: A. R. Mowbray and Company, 1969.

Peters, Victor. *All Things Common: the Hutterian Way of Life.* New York: Harper and Row, 1971.

Plowman, Edward E. *The Jesus Movement in America.* Elgin, Ill.: David C. Cook, 1971.

Potts, Margaret I. *St. Julian's: An Experiment in Two Continents.* London: SCM Press, 1968.

Praeger, Lydia, editor. *Frei für Gott und die Menschen.* Stuttgart: Quell-Verlag, 1964.

Reffold, A. E. *Wilson Carlile and the Church Army.* London: Church Army Bookshop, 1956.

Richardson, Herbert W. *Nun, Witch, Playmate.* New York: Harper and Row, 1971.

Robertson, Constance Noyes. *Oneida Community: The Breakup.* Syracuse, N.Y.: Syracuse University Press, 1972.

Sams, Henry W. *Autobiography of Brook Farm.* Englewood Cliffs, N.J.: Prentice-Hall, 1958.

Schaeffer, Edith. *L'Abri.* Wheaton: Tyndale House Publishers, 1969.

Schlink, Klara (Mother Basilea). *God Is Always Greater.* Foreword by Olive Wyon. London: Faith Press, 1963.

–––. *Realities.* Grand Rapids: Zondervan Publishing House, 1969.

–––. *When God Calls.* Minneapolis: Bethany Fellowship, 1970.

Schutz, Roger. *Living Today for God.* Translated by Stephen McNierney and Louis Evrad. Baltimore: Helicon Press, 1961.

Shamburgh, H. *Amana: The Community of True Inspiration.* Iowa City, Iowa: State Historical Society of Iowa, 1908.

Stoeffler, F. Ernest. *The Rise of Evangelical Pietism.* Leiden: E. J. Brill, 1965.

Synan, Vinson. *The Holiness-Pentecostal Movement.* Grand Rapids: Wm. B. Eerdmans Publishing Company, 1971.

Teselle, Sallie, editor. *The Family, Communes and Utopian Societies.* New York: Harper Torchbooks, 1973.

Thurian, Max. *Consecration of the Layman.* Baltimore: Helicon Press, 1963.

———. *Marriage and Celibacy.* Translated by Norma Emerton. London: Student Christian Movement Press, Ltd., 1959.

Trueblood, Elton. *Signs of Hope in a Century of Despair.* New York: Harper and Brothers, 1950.

Vasto, Lanza del. *Return to the Source.* New York: Schocken Books, 1971. [By the founder of the Order of the Ark.]

Verwer, George. *Come! Live! Die!* Wheaton: Tyndale, 1973.

Wakefield, Gordon, *Puritan Devotion.* London: Epworth Press, 1957.

Ward, Hiley H. *The Far-Out Saints of the Jesus Communes.* New York: Association Press, 1972.

Webber, Everett. *Escape to Utopia.* New York: Hastings House, 1959.

Weiser, Frederick S. *Love's Response.* Philadelphia: Board of Publication of the United Lutheran Church in America, 1962.

———. *The Survival of Monastic Life in Post-Reformation Lutheranism.* S.T.M. thesis. Gettysburg, Penn.: Lutheran Theological Seminary, 1966.

Wilson, William E. *The Angel and the Serpent: The Story of New Harmony.* Bloomington, Ind.: Indiana University Press, 1964.

Winslow, Jack. *The Lee Abbey Story.* London: Lutterworth Press, 1956.

Wyon, Olive. *Living Springs.* Philadelphia: Westminster Press, 1963.

Yamura, Barbara. *A Change and a Parting: My Story of Amana.* Ames: Iowa State University Press, 1960.

Zablocki, Benjamin J. *The Joyful Community.* Baltimore: Penguin Books, 1971. [On the Bruderhof.]

Index of Names

Aaron   23
Abraham   23
Allshorn, Florence   68, 69, 114
Anson, Peter   47, 114
Aquinas, Thomas   24, 25
Arnold, Emmy   114
Asbury, Francis   42
Augustine   31

Bach, Marcus   49
Balthasar, Hans Urs von   25
Barnabas   22
Barth, Karl   107
Baxter, Richard   38
Beissal, Johann Conrad   40, 116
Benedict of Nursia   37
Bengel, Johann Albrecht   38
Berg, David   88, 89
Bernardino of Siena   103
Biot, Francois   36, 112, 114
Blumhardt, Christoph   8, 108
Bodelschwingh, Friedrich von
   47, 115
Bonhoeffer, Dietrich   82, 99,
   100, 114
Booth, William   107
Bosanquet, Mary   99, 100
Bromiley, G. W.   107
Brown, Harold   93
Bunyan, John   38

Calvin, John   28, 29, 99
Carmichael, Amy   43
Cassian, John   24
Cochrane, Arthur   32

Day, Dorothy   27, 116

Drakeford, John W.   115
Drolet, Francis   115
Durnbaugh, Donald F.   115

Eckhart, Meister   26, 28, 30
Edwards, Jonathan   38
England, Martin   78

Fénelon, Francois   30
Ferguson, Charles   115
Ferrar, Nicholas   39
Finney, Charles   84
Forsyth, Peter T.   103
Foucauld, Charles de   101
Francke, August   38, 39

Gennuvit, Jean   39
Graham, Billy   45

Halkenhäuser, Johann   58
Hammarskjöld, Dag   99
Harnack, Adolf   34
Harris, Howell   42
Hegre, Theodore   83, 84, 115
Hümmer, Hanna   61
Hümmer, Walter   59, 61, 108

Isaac   23
Isaiah   22, 82

Jacob   23, 82
Jeremiah   22
Jerome   24
John the Baptist   22, 23
Jordan, Clarence   78, 81, 116
Joseph of Arimathea   23

Kelpius, Johann   39
Kierkegaard, Soren   33, 34

119

Index of Subjects

DATE DUE